Sabbatical Reflections

Sabbatical Reflections

THE TEN COMMANDMENTS IN A NEW DAY

Brita Stendahl

FORTRESS PRESS
Philadelphia

First published 1980

COPYRIGHT © 1980 BY BRITA STENDAHL

Library of Congress Cataloging in Publication Data

Stendahl, Brita K
    Sabbatical reflections.

    1. Commandments, Ten. 2. Christian life—Lutheran authors. 3. Stendahl, Brita K. I. Title.
BV4655.S74   248 '.4   79-23775
ISBN 0-8006-0643-4

8525D80   Printed in the United States of America   1-643

For Krister

CONTENTS

INTRODUCTION

Each year there is an exodus of American academic families. East and West they break up from home, take children out of school, sublet their houses, pack the necessary books and the few changes of clothing that the airlines will allow them and set out on the adventure called "the sabbatical leave." Each year there is an equal number returning. When asked by colleagues and neighbors, "How was your year?" They answer, "Wonderful." And as they begin to describe it the neighbor and friend soon gets confused by foreign names, problems with schoolboards, mix-ups in shops, unbelievable plumbing conditions, recalcitrant librarians, etc., and, as human nature has it, begins to tell his or her own experience of moving. Thus the equalization process begins to level the experience and all gets back to normal. Eventually a book is published where the sabbatical is recalled in a short sentence expressing grateful thanks for the opportunity.

❦

From these brief encounters with enthusiastic colleagues and by perusing their results, solidified in book form, new generations of scholars build their image of what a sabbatical leave should yield and set out themselves on the sabbatical journey with high hopes and expectations. They return and few there are who admit that the sabbatical was less than they expected. The time it took just to cope was collossal, to manage the organization, let alone the improvement of one's work habits in a strange environment. To deal in a foreign language caused constant uneasiness. The homesickness of the children produced guilt feelings and daily training in consolation. The book that was going to be the visible result of the year faded with every incoming week, producing writer's cramp. Since these experiences never are recounted in forewords and grateful acknowledgements, they are not part of the legend. Few reflect upon the fact that the shining halo around the sabbatical leave is polished by those scholars who were unimaginative or wise enough to turn to the familiar during their year of leisure. Secure in the familiar, be it language, region, or library, they could enjoy the unfamiliar as ponderable quirks of culture.

9

This is of course the reason why some professors nowadays decide not to go away during their sabbatical leave but stay in the thoroughly familiar, just shutting themselves off from all commitments except those to their own work.

I am not out to judge what or how is the best way to spend a sabbatical year. We had one in 1959–60 which we spent together with our children in Sweden, our native country. For me it was a thoroughly happy year. For the children that year was not easy, but in retrospect it became the time in their life when they reacquainted themselves with the Swedish language and with "roots" as we like to say nowadays. For Krister, my husband, a theologian, who had kept his contacts with the Swedish theological faculties and church life in Sweden, it was a year of frustrating reentry. Looking back, none of us think of that year as a year of leisure.

Burned by the difficulties our children had had, we were not to pull them out of their schools again when the next sabbatical came around in 1967–68. This time we were going to try the staying-home model. I was teaching, the children went to school, the house went through the seasons and sprung a leak in the unusually icy winter. Krister sat at his desk or paced the floor in his study to which the doors were closed.

Seven years later, during the academic year of 1974–75, we were again ready for a leave. This time it was all different. No problem with resettling the children. They were now grown-up, independent, and married. We were on our own. A whole year lay ahead of us. We divided the time so that we first lived for four months out on Nantucket in our summer home. There we tied up loose ends, finishing up work whose deadlines were slipping by. The mornings at the desk, the afternoons pottering about the house, the garden, and the neighborhood.

At the end of October when the air got chilly and the unheated house constantly reminded us that it was time to leave, the manuscripts were sent off and we left. Unburdened by commitments, we packed four suitcases, of which two contained the travel library, and flew to Sweden where we spent the following four months out in a farmhouse situated conveniently on the plains of Uppland at an hour's distance from Stockholm, where our relatives live, and half an hour away from Uppsala, where we had studied and where we still have many friends.

Our next chunk of time was to be devoted to travel. We had been able to purchase Eurail-passes that would allow us to roam freely around Europe for three months. We wrote to friends and colleagues and Krister lined up a string of lectures. At the beginning of March we were off to meet the Spring in the south of Europe.

It was the coldest Spring in memory. Already at the beginning of May we were back in Sweden, anxious to gather together the spoils of our labors and pack it into shape at the desk. A very hard task and a test. May 15th became a memorable, decisive day of which I will speak later. May became the turning point in our string of leisurely months. When June arrived we were ready and eager to return to the United States and begin work again, to assume responsibilities, accept appointments, and see the calendar fill up.

The year itself had been a full experience. When people asked, "How was your sabbatical?" I felt poor in just answering, "Wonderful!" and many times wished I could mould it into solid form and put it as an artifact on our mantelpiece telling people, "Look at our sabbatical, isn't she beautiful!"

Perhaps it is valid to say that this book became that artifact. The content was there when we returned. It consisted of the kind of writing I do when an incident, a remark, an article, or a memory triggers my mind, refuses to go away, and blocks me from continuing writing what I am working on for the moment. I then switch the paper in the typewriter. Often the new sheet by its sheer whiteness scares my new-found thoughts. They peter out and look so pitiful that I soon lay the paper aside. During the sabbatical I did more of that sort of piecemeal writing, but the sheer bulk I produced prohibited me from throwing it away. Here was something tangible and perhaps worth saving.

But it was still only material in search of form and thus it went into storage. Two years later I took it out and began picking at it, discarding some and adding some. But it was still unwieldy. Had it been a travelogue or a memoir, then the organizing principle would have been easy to hit upon. Chronology offers its convenience, but these scraps of paper were dealing with something else, sometimes repetitiously so: What is it to be in-between? What does it mean to live in-between two countries, two cultures, two ages? How and where to find one's bearings? In snippets these pages speak about what it was like to be a middle-aged, middle-class, immigrant woman in the 1970s. The seventies will perhaps be remembered as the decade in search of values when all the things we used to do and all we took for granted was up for reevaluation. It is when we are in-between that we have to return to basics.

During the beginning of the sabbatical I made ready for publication a book on Sören Kierkegaard and then during our months in Sweden I checked out and read Fredrika Bremer, Sweden's first female novelist, as a possible subject for my next book. These two authors, though different in the extreme, were both pious and aware of the consequences of piety. My thoughts hovered over theirs while old concepts presented themselves in new form: life as pilgrimage, life as in-between; life in God as happiness; sin as the unhappiness of human relationships. What does it mean to obey God more? Thus I hit upon the Ten Commandments as a formula for organization.

For Jews and Christians the Ten Commandments are basic measures against which we test our performance, our adherence to the will of God. As the times change, so do the demands. Not until I got the idea to order the material around the commandments did it take shape and find unity. My awareness of the fundamental importance and pressure of the commandments made me see why I, at times, had been so eager to put a blank paper in my typewriter. I was prompted by uncertainty rather than certainty. A question was on its way to find an answer.

Thus form and content came together. The reader may still find it rather loose but, as far as I am concerned, it is finished and ready to be put on the shelf. It might not be as beautiful as I had hoped, but it is significant inasmuch as it reveals where I was during the mid-1970s.

Finally, then, the question: Is it not rather too personal? Having studied Kierkegaard I am aware of the importance of the question, and the answer I give is both a yes and a no. In the past I have reflected on the difference between male and female traditions of writing. I look forward to that day when male and female will have liberated each other, so that men will not be afraid to reveal their personal experiences when they speak out and women no longer will be timid or intimidated to limit themselves to safe female experiences, but will, from that perspective, enter the whole range of human complexities. What a day that will be! And not far off.

CHAPTER 1

You Shall Have No Other Gods Before Me

On Columbus Day in 1954, I was standing at the ship's railing with my two children holding onto my skirt—all three of us feeling uncomfortable in heavy tweed suits, while the sun was pouring down. We were nevertheless predictably awed by the magnificent sight of Manhattan. We were totally unaware that we were now about to play a part in the long, tortuous, heroic drama of American immigration. We thought we were just coming on a visit, but we were, in reality, being drawn into a modern phase of immigration.

Krister had been called to Harvard for a two years' visiting professorship. He had flown ahead of us to make arrangements, to rent an apartment, and buy some furniture.

He would be at the pier to meet us. Manhattan grew hazy from the sudden Indian-summer heat wave and New York humidity. The immigration process seemed interminably long due to our pent-up anxiety before an unknown future. Our voyage had been delayed by the unusual Fall storms of hurricane strength. When finally processed, we descended to a dirty, crowded, and busy pier. The children were restive and sweating in their blue Harris tweed. We looked around for our belongings which we were to find under the letter *S*. Finally we caught sight of Krister coming smiling towards us, already assimilated, with a crew cut and dressed in slacks, a thin white shirt, and sandals. With him at our side, the entrance became painless.

We stopped at a Howard Johnson's for dinner. Its plastic was gleaming and shining clean in bright colors. The children's menu made us laugh. We arrived in Cambridge late that weekend on Columbus Day, but it is only in retrospect that the fact takes on symbolic meaning. It did not occur to me at all during those days that we were part of a movement. Of course we knew about Swedish emigration to America, since most Swedes have at least one distant relative in the United States. Krister is one of the few who does not, but I have two uncles and their families in Iowa: one had left Sweden to avoid the draft and the other, to find employment. We were not like them. We did not even think of making comparisons.

That we were "drafted" never occurred to me. We were one tiny family out of thousands who came to the United States after the war, at the bidding of universities and other institutions. This new kind of emigration—very different from the old one and yet so similar in consequence—was called the "brain drain." It was already resented by some, both in Sweden and in the United States, but its numbers (compared to, for example, the Puerto-Rican immigration) were still so insignificant. We were always treated with such grace, friendliness, and partiality that the immigrant fact took many years to sink in.

Columbus came to the New World ill-informed but with the ambition to conquer and return home laden with goods. In Henry James's *The American*, a French lady remarks quite aptly that Columbus "invented" rather than "discovered" America. From Columbus's and Europe's point of view, this is, of course, correct. What native Americans thought is another matter.

Our family began right away to discover and invent America. We plunged into what Krister, in retrospect, calls "Stage 1" of immigration, the curiosity phase. This is when one notices all that is different, all that is wrong according to the standards one has unconsciously brought along. Now the Swedish measuring stick came out, and there was a lot to criticize and question in American society. Yet we were much amused at the aura of innocence, the air of confidence in people's belief that they lived in the greatest country on earth. Whenever we raised questions we got ourselves an earful of answers. True, there were racial problems, for instance, but the government, the law, and the courts were on the side of the oppressed. This was certainly not South Africa. Since we never met any Black people socially during those first years, we never heard the other side.

The social differences were explained to us. The system of free enterprise had created a gap between the rich and the poor. Since, however, the stream of immigrants always had supplied the country with poor, illiterate laborers, the poor were here to stay and would always be among us. The glory of America was that it provided opportunity. If someone has what it takes, he would rise from his humble station. We trusted this explanation, since we never met any poor people, except the "academic slum" to which we ourselves belonged; this was a cheerful group that looked forward to tenure. Somewhere. America has an enormous number of educational institutions. We saw people come and go, always courteous, always interesting individuals and seemingly almost void of personal envy. There were plenty of opportunities.

Certainly we noticed the incredible inequalities in social welfare. If one could pay or establish credit, one would receive the best medical care, the smartest lawyers, and the loveliest options as a consumer. Since we were considered good risks, we got in on this deal and we and our friends never smarted under the common phenomenon of being cheated. When we heard about such cases and discussed them, the belief in the goodness of the people and the justice of the law asserted itself as strong as the future itself. We thought to ourselves, this inequity will pass and the situation will inevitably improve.

In this way we were quickly moving into "Stage 2" in the immigration process, the adjustment phase. Soon we heard ourselves repeat to other newcomers these very words of explanation in defense of the great experiment in coexistence that is America. And our children (who by that time were settled in school and in the habits of their comrades) strengthened this stage by absolutely adoring the freer life-style of American children. America was a children's paradise. Children were provided through TV with entertainment, through the automobile with mobility, through snackbars with their favorite foods, through dime stores with innumerable opportunities to spend their pocket money on stuff they could afford. "Stage 2," the stage of the "American dream," had us in its firm grip when we returned to Sweden in 1959–60, on Krister's first sabbatical leave. Everything at home seemed small, defined, and confined. People spoke and thought in terms of security and had developed a society that provided maximum safeguards for the Swedes. We were put to it through constant discussions to try to enlarge the Swedish thinking to include plurality. And I am afraid that we said over and over, "In America . . ."

As so many bourgeois Swedish families did during the first part of this century, our family looked upon the United States with great fondness and admiration for its youth and vigor, generosity and strength. During and immediately following World War II, the popularity of the United States reached its height. We compared the way Russia emptied its satellite countries of goods with the generous way America pumped money and food into Germany, thus laying the foundation for the *Wirtschaftswunder*. We in the West had very little knowledge and not enough empathy to understand that Russia at that time was desperately poor and hungry, economically smashed by the war. We just did not expect Russia to be generous. We found satisfaction for our bias in seeing that East Germany was drab and grey, while West Germany prospered.

Germany was close to Sweden, and therefore we could follow its development. We were ignorant, however, about what had happened elsewhere, especially in the Far East. To most Swedes the war was over in 1945. We hardly realized that the Americans had been fighting not only the Germans but also the Japanese. The whole Pacific "Theatre," as it was called, was just that: a play taking place somewhere far off—too far off for comprehension. The Korean War did not become a reality to most Europeans and, if anything, it enhanced our image of the generous Americans gallantly taking on the battle against Communism, a cause most popular in a Socialist Sweden which, for centuries, had feared Russia and now feared her all the more with Stalin at the helm. We knew vaguely that America had its troubles and problems and we had read *An American Dilemma*, but our trust was unshakeable that these problems would be overcome in a country which spoke so well and fought so energetically for democracy and which had such a splendid Bill of Rights.

We were hardly back in the United States before we fell right into "Stage 3," the phase of integration. We had just left a stable society that provided for all its citizens and which was almost free from corruption. With this fresh in our memory we looked upon American society with new eyes. We began to take stock of our own heritage, ponder it, compare it, be fair but depend on our own judgment. It took us twelve years of living in America to decide whether we ought to take out papers to apply for citizenship. And when we took that step, it was not the "American dream" that prompted us; it was the Vietnam War.

Why is it that on this, our third sabbatical, we again have to go through the arguments for and against the ordination of women? This time we listen to the arguments coming from the students who seem so young because we have grown old. For me it is tragic to hear these students, fresh out of high school, repeat the same arguments that I heard my father refute in the 1940s, my husband debate in the 1950s, and which I have seen so many women deny and defy by their word and deed since the 1960s. Finally, in these last years, in our own church in Cambridge, we have had these arguments eradicated by the successful co-ministry of a man and a woman. But— back in Uppsala—here we go again.

In 1958 the Church Assembly voted to admit women to the priesthood. Now there are many women priests in almost all the thirteen Swedish dioceses and more seem to be coming. But when we listen today to the kind of persecution these female theologians have to endure from some of their male colleagues, one would think that it was yesterday that the idea was born, the vote was taken, the books written, and the women had all been ordained in one swoop of erratic enthusiasm, and today is the morning after.

It has dawned on me that when I studied theology no other woman was credited with more importance that the mythical Eve. The place of Mary was never strongly stressed in our Lutheran heritage. Women in the Bible and women in church history were not highlighted on reading lists or in exam questions. Neither can I remember that it ever was mentioned or reflected upon that most congregations were in the main made up of women. To what extent did all wonderful theological meditation have an impact on the women who flocked to the door of the church? Did they agree? Were they convinced? What made them come? Were they merely superstitious or was there some genuine education going on? What did they negotiate to their children? The one and only Swede who made it to canonical rank was a woman, a formidable woman who quarrelled with the pope, founded her own order, and put down her own rule. Birgitta. My parents named me after her but did I ever learn to understand her? No!

We learned of course that Abraham was married to Sarah (with Hagar in the wings), Isaac to Rebekah, Jacob to Rachel and Leah. Augustine's mother was the lachrymose, persistent Monica and Luther's hefty wife was Catherine, but these women were incidental appendices as far as theological textbooks were concerned. Not until I belatedly arrived at Sören Kierkegaard and learned about Regine, a woman who was truly accidental in his life, did Kierkegaard's con-

stant reflection upon that meeting stir my consciousness to an awareness of the hitherto almost perfectly repressed presence of women in
the whole of history. This made history again interesting because it
opened a completely new field for research. The subordination of
women, what has it done to men? The suppression of the awareness
of woman's work, what has it done to recorded history? The
cooperation of women, what has it meant for the church? The
opposition of women, what claim has it on the formation of sects?
I would like to begin my studies anew.

What I am after—I am not quite sure what to call it. The word
spirituality is what first comes to mind. What was the spirituality of
the women who thronged in the cloisters? What was the spirituality
of the women who fostered the greats? What influence, if any, did
the great have on the spirituality of their wives and vice versa?
I know, the word I want is not spirituality, but *piety*.

Spirituality makes me envision hymnals, prayer books, candles,
and silent meditation. But I want to find these people in mind and
body. Who were the women who carried food to the hermits, who
married the sungods, who agreed to temple prostitution, who cared
for dying Vincent St. Paul, who followed Brigham Young, and
who carried out all these tasks with such dignity and conviction
that legends were told and traditions were wrought? Less spectacularly
but nevertheless an important question, the answer to which would
teach us a lot about the human race: Why do women go to church?
What is the secret of their piety? And why is "piety" and "pious" for
so many an ugly and shameful thing today?

Why the word *piety*?

In the *Encyclopedia Brittanica*, which I have at my elbow, *piety*
is defined as (1) reverence towards God or the gods; religious devout-
ness; (2) religiousness in general; (3) filial honor and obedience as due
to parents, superiors, or country. According to this definition we
are all pious to a greater or lesser degree, depending on our consciousness. We all behave and feel on cue. Out of decorum we act or refuse
to act according to how we interpret the ceremony. Many who will
have nothing to do with religious services, especially the communion,
would travel hundreds of miles for a baseball game or turkey on
Thanksgiving and mother's pumpkin pie. The gut feeling we have for
what is good, lovable, and strengthening!

Piety should be examined—not in order to be discarded, because it cannot be discarded, but in order to find out what we really value and what we have outgrown and outworn. Piety itself is not hurt thereby. Piety grows from inside and it thrives on being pruned. Though vulnerable for a while it also grows stronger and fresher. Feelings towards God, parents, and country may and should change with our new words about them. Our words about them and our deeds towards them alter all through life but nothing is lost, just cleansed.

It isn't preposterous to speak in such nebulous generalities. Nevertheless that is the mode of sabbatical philosophy. With a travesty on Hume I could say, "Be a philosopher but above all be a woman." Relaxed, thinking like a "normal" person grasping for words to express what I see, feel, hear, and, yes, smell. Don't stop now! You don't have to be scholarly. Scholarship is always afterthought, tidying up, ordering discovery.

Piety begins on the gut-feeling level. It runs through many stages all the way to, say, the Quakers' "inner light." Important as it is to distinguish the difference, it is equally important to remember the connection. It is the connection that plays into the question of the ordination of women, for instance.

Thus piety is not theology. To do theology is to try to think and formulate "the thoughts of God." To study theology is to examine how people have tried to do this in the past. Piety on the other hand is our human answer. Our instant reflex towards desire, dream, threats, utopia—on cue in a given situation. It can be unconscious or half-conscious or fully conscious.

Piety is the human response. In the centuries preceding the twentieth, people would have had no trouble with the word. But today, because it is almost tied in with the exclusively religious, a great many people, especially in Sweden, go to great length in declaring that they are in no way pious. The Swedes, though, are exceedingly pious in their adherence to "civility," rules laid down by their forefathers. Olle Hedberg, a Swedish author, scratched at that surface of bourgeois civility in all his works to reveal the "hidden fears, the envy, greed, and guilt." Perhaps that is why people considered him nasty and have downgraded him as a writer. He touched something very close to home, a style for which there was reverence much akin with ancestor worship.

For some people to do what always has been done and answer yes to the demands of family and society becomes, for various reasons, not enough. It jars with what they consider their honesty. Their energy craves more. Their anxiety grows. They must find their special task, their mission in life. Once they have found their cause there is no way of stopping them before they have spent themselves. Here is common ground for Kierkegaard and Bremer, however much they otherwise differ.

Self-fulfillment is the goal of much striving in our modern times, a goal very different from the one heralded by preachers, hymnals, postillae, and consolata of earlier periods. To their beckoning one answered in an unreflected way with good deeds, with prayer, with tears of sorrow and joy, and with steadfastness, faithfulness to the Word, forgiveness and humility. Self-fulfillment can mean money, career, women, men, children, honor—in short, what is driving us, piety pursued with aggression. Piety has, of course, to do with sexuality. The strength of our response lies not merely in education but within our genes, within the body. That is the secret of its persistence and capriciousness. Our body is a mystery to us. It traps our reason. The centuries created a great divide between heavenward piety and hellbent desire. In earnest prayer people confessed their earthly desires and asked for deliverance against themselves. But vitality has to do with sexuality and energy, a kind of burner in the center of our being. This precious energy forms us while we are growing up and sustains us as grown-ups. Its warmth helps us to endure, forget, and forgive because we are attached and asking for renewed relationship. Our happiness and unhappiness depend upon our ways of severing and rebounding our relatedness. We depend on this seed planted within us and on how we are nurtured and how we nurture and foster this seed.

Now I understand better why, as a young woman, I liked the words by the Swedish poet Gunnar Ekelöf:

Honor the senses in your body
and in the bodies of those who give to yours its share:
Sex, the one thing in you and them able to grow
the seed the gods deposited

An unselfish flower will then, perhaps, shoot forth
Since only there is a cranny
a chink in the wall:
Pyramus et Thisbe—Philemon and Baucis
Don't smile at the simple myth, not even at the superficial one
since it may become your own at the blackest sea

The subconscious is wise
If you're occupied with it, don't interpret
Obey! In dream and impulse
the soul like the plant builds new leaves

Do not translate a living language into a dead
Honor the mysterium of your body-soul
And thus be edified

Kierkegaard, who thought of most things and thought of them in an unconventional manner, returning again and again to the same themes to check and doublecheck, got hold of this. He lived, however, at a time when perhaps we had the greatest disparity between divine reason and sinful lust. If the sensual is banned as sin, this leads to a stimulation of the sexual imagination and intensifies the dread of the sexual. Kierkegaard makes this very clear in his book *The Concept of Dread,* where he expounds on the idea that it is Christianity which makes sexuality sinful. The religious has suspended the erotic in Christianity not only through an ethical misunderstanding by calling it sinful, but also through making it indifferent since in the spirit there is no difference between man and woman. "The erotic is not here made neutral through irony but is suspended because it is the nature of Christianity to move the spirit forward. Through shame the spirit becomes shy and frightened of the generic difference and the individuality is broken and instead of finding a place in the ethical it stretches for something higher to get an explanation." The problem Kierkegaard was wrestling with was the consequences of the exclusion of sex in Christianity by considering it a matter of indifference. Through exclusion it had gained vicious power and returned with vengeance to maul the spirit.

Kierkegaard's psychology reveals endless insights into the interplay between despair and sin (*The Sickness Unto Death*) and also into the power of love (*The Works of Love*): the difficulty for a human being to receive life from the Creator instead of insisting on creating it oneself; the enormous hindrance and humiliation to man to let something happen to him instead of going ahead on his own aggressive speed. Love is life's hidden base and an irresistible need, yet to receive love from God is the hardest task for a human being. Kierkegaard tried to make it understood through his maieutic method that love runs counter to original sin, shame, and despair. Love is present in one's neighbor as in oneself as something preconscious which is waiting and eager to be fulfilled. But this love needs edification to dare live in a Christlike manner or it gets stuck and overthrown by selfishness.

Although they were contemporaries and both were independently wealthy and knew many of the same people and had read many of the same books and both were serious about their Christianity, Sören Kierkegaard and Fredrika Bremer are totally different. She was a woman. Her mother's highest ambition was to get her daughter married according to status and upbringing. Fredrika Bremer wanted differently though she really did not know what. There were no models. As a child she wanted to fight for king and country and ran away to join the army. Her teachers taught her to dance, draw, sew, play the piano, and to read and speak many languages. But what use was she going to have of that were she not to marry? Fumblingly she began to walk her own way. At first secretly, and then openly she published stories that were so well received that she tried the novel form. She was pleased that people liked what she wrote but she was not satisfied. There must be something more, something she was missing. At every turn she felt how deficient her education had been. She engaged a teacher to introduce her to philosophy and theology. She was lucky. Per Böklin not only got a dutiful student, he got a pupil who had an insatiable appetite for questioning everything between heaven and earth and he responded with understanding, amazement, perseverance, and all the knowledge and insight that he had. Later she thanked him for having created a cosmos out of her chaos. But he did more than that. Gently he led her to faith; a miracle for Fredrika Bremer who felt that life opened up and her engagement in it became vital. Just at that point, however, Böklin, unsensitive to what was happening to her and enamored with her capacity for love, proposed to her. This threw her into turmoil. Just as Kierkegaard she felt then that she could not marry. She had a higher calling than entering into wedlock. She was on a search that could not be curtailed and for which she needed her full independence. Thus it came about that these two authors who sing the praise of the happy marriage both recoiled from entering the marital state. Somehow they knew in their guts that it would not work, that they needed their independence for something other.

Kierkegaard reflected forever on that choice. Not so Fredrika Bremer. She began to move both physically and spiritually. The past had very little to offer, but God was at work and his new reality which was to include women in a new manner had to be found. When Fredrika Bremer traveled to the United States it was very much in her mind that she should study the American home, where women were free and creative together with the men in a way very different from Europe. The main sin in her homeland was the submission of women and their incarceration in traditional homes. The title of the book where she reports on her travels in America signified her aim, *The Homes in the New World.*

Fredrika Bremer meets people open-faced. She is not stupid or undiscerning. She comes to know herself. She never frets that people do not appreciate her. She walks her way undaunted, trusting God. She has fought hard to win her faith but after it was won she lives in it, protected by it as by a transparent, invisible shield.

Piety is at work when a new situation occurs. Then one is caught unawares, overwhelmed by a multitude of unconscious memories from experiences in the past and one's feelings rise accordingly. Reason is always two steps behind. Individuality and relatedness support each other. If relatedness has been disturbed or halted severely once, it is likely to be difficult to get the flow back again.

Patriarchal religion depicts God as an imperial ruler who demands obedience. One can wonder if the women listening to sermons preached in this vein felt this as pressure. The dichotomy between body and soul helped to create the patriarchal exploitation of woman. The soul, the mind, and the spirit became the more important and the more refined elements over which men had understanding and exclusive command, while women were relegated to the physical world, the realm of the body, the instinctual, the sentimental. It is typical when women writers emerge, that they are labeled "realists" and "sentimentalists." These women had never forgotten that a person's relationship to the body is organic necessity. What they tried to depict was often either the desperate feeling of being trapped or the exhilaration of being able to transcend the givenness of the body. The problem was an obvious one. While women knew of their immense dependence on men and wanted that relationship to be addressed and redressed with mutual honesty, equality, and respect, men enjoyed and took for granted their superiority and independence. The more fragile their situation became with the emancipation of women, the more they felt threatened and the harder they tried to emphasize and spiritualize the differences between male and female.

Strindberg is a wonderful example of this development. In his first book on *Marriage* he is a perfectly sound and witty paternalistic man, but in the second book, *Marriage II*, written when he had been badly hurt and threatened, he is a vicious misogynist.

In the 1970s we ought not to have any difficulty with the question concerning the ordination of women. We have thought about it, voted it through, seen it happen, met these devoted ministers, heard them preach, and participated in their services. But some devout Christians just refuse to have anything to do with them. Traditional piety hangs on. There is something more comforting to people about God, the Father, than God, the Mother. That God created human beings in his image as men and women does not make an impact. Some people find the male image so much more reassuring.

"You shall have no other God before me" is an awesome but wonderful commandment, because it forces us to reexamine whether we have got stuck, whether we have old idols instead of a living God. When we reexamine our piety we do well to remember the body and its memories. A living person is the product of the flow of experience. God speaks to the whole person.

CHAPTER 2

You Shall Not Take the Name of the Lord in Vain

When we arrived in Cambridge my then six-year-old son was given a cowboy outfit. He asked for ammunition for his guns. I looked up the Swedish word for "ammunition" in the dictionary and wrote down the English equivalent on a piece of paper and told him to show the paper to the manager of the local toy store. After quite some time he returned and looked at me with utter scorn. "Demolition powder," he muttered. So I asked, "Did you get your *knallpulver?* —the 'demolition powder' I had written on the slip of paper?" "Mother," he said, and from the way he said it I could imagine the scene down at the store, "the word is caps, C-A-P-S."

The dictionary certainly is an inroad to another language, but it does not take us all the way. At times it may even stop the communication we wish to establish. It is dangerous, we know, to confuse "lust" with "desire." But aside from running the risk of making mistakes, we are making fools of ourselves either by over-stating or by blurring our intent. Dictionary definitions may help us articulate, but in so doing we might also articulate our peculiarity.

The South American scholar who told us that "his salary was very few" certainly made a grammatical mistake, but he also made us see him and realize that what he said was probably true. He was not well paid. Unlike a Harvard professor or a German or Swedish professor, he did not enjoy status and prestige and a stable income in his country.

One of the most rewarding experiences in any language is to be able to tell stories and enjoy their effect on listeners. For years, however, our children begged us, "Please, don't tell Swedish stories; Swedish humor is awful." They gave us the impression that Swedes do not have any humor or that their humor is coarse and clumsy. It took me quite a long time to understand that the stories we thought were amusing needed quite a lot more than just dictionary translation to be rendered funny.

The moment you are able to tell a story in another language and get spontaneous laughter in response, then you can be proud of having taken a big step forward on the brittle bridge of communication. Your feel for setting, tradition, and timing has found appropriate expression.

As most immigrants we picked up colloquial terms at first, because they attracted our attention and we found them colorful and fun. But that was a treacherous road. To be able to use colloquialisms you must first master correct speech. The natives immediately detect where you stand on the ladder of competence in their language. If you begin to spew colloquial expressions while still hanging on to the lowest rung, then people are not long amused, but embarrassed. If you have not yet acquired a style, then you cannot break a style, which is the purpose for the use of colloquialisms.

As the years progressed we learned. Krister learned much faster than I. For that matter he learned far faster than anyone I have ever observed. It used to depress me that it seemed so easy for him to find the right expression. That was not all, but he was able to turn a phrase in such a way that people listened and responded. Two-way traffic started. Sometimes, when I dared interrupt with a comment, I got the feeling that my input was an intrusion; we must have this obstacle cleared away as fast as possible in order to continue the communication train.

After I had been teaching for a while, I started to understand what was going on. The interested and intelligent students picked up much more than what I had actually said. They sat there and filled in the gaps, savored the flavor of something which perhaps had not been intended, and they wove their own network. When they interrupted, they increased and widened the scope. Teaching became great fun because it meant catching up and reaching out. In terms of this integrating stage on the road into a new language, it was a pity that my teaching job petered out. I noticed very soon thereafter how I regressed and was back to my awkward side comments. Being isolated all day with my own thoughts, I found it impossible suddenly to hit the right note when brought before a crowd that had no image of me and little interest in what I said.

"Do you think, count, dream, address your children in English or in Swedish?" These are questions people ask me all the time; they are not easy to answer right away. As soon as we arrived in the

United States we began to speak English at home; we wanted to facilitate the transfer for the children. Thinking that we were to stay only a short two-year period, we wanted to become as familiar as we possibly could with the English language. The children, of course, didn't approve in the beginning: why try a strange language when you have one you are comfortable with? But they learned quickly and it was not long before they were embarrassed by how we expressed ourselves and by our Swedish accent. The children corrected us and we heeded them as far as we were able. They learned to read, count, sing, skip, and dream in English. Their Swedish receded but it surfaced when we visited Sweden or when relatives or guests came from Sweden to visit us.

Now I sometimes think in English and sometimes in Swedish. To keep one language totally separate from the other is nearly impossible. Between us, Krister and I have a mixture which is understood only by us. In this language of no country I dream, talk to myself, and, at times, absentmindedly to others. This mixture, understood only by Krister, is probably what will be left with me in my advanced and calcified age. To be bilingual is an impossibility if the requirement is purity. English is too rich; Swedish is too powerful; we are too impatient.

"And where do you come from?" After having lived such a long time in a country, I feel that it is humiliating to have that question repeatedly thrown at me in the middle of an interesting conversation. Humiliating but also thought-provoking. Bilingualism, the dream of many scholars and the aim of many experiments, is a thing of poverty and riches. As far as is humanly possible, Krister is now bilingual, and I am not too far behind. The children have English as their first language, but they speak and understand Swedish without difficulty, so we have all achieved something that was once aspired.

❦

What were the people dreaming of then? A world community where people were as fish in the water, swimming along without the obstacle of languages? A peaceful world of understanding where explanations were easily found? It is lovely to be in an international setting where interpreters are not always needed, but as soon as we encounter Russian, Japanese, Chinese, or even Spanish, we are lost, and we are equally lost with Irish factory workers, Scottish fishermen,

American farmworkers, or migrant grape pickers. A bilingual professor can speak to other professors, but can he talk to all his compatriots? This, of course, depends on his or her humanity, because it is not so that other groups are without language or endowed with less. On the contrary, language in those groups is more potent since it is used less flippantly. My grandmother used to say, "Don't play with words." Words have a meaning built over the years; a delicate building should be respected, not demolished.

ꙮ

Words. When we came to this country we heard words, words, words, and our whole beings had to stretch to make sense out of what we heard and to make ourselves understand. It made me ache as after gymnastics, and I became very tired. I took a nap every day in the beginning of our stay. I despaired and thought that I would never be able to grasp what was said on the radio. I would iron and listen to the radio with tears falling down my cheeks because I could not make sense of the garble I heard. Every day I did a small amount of laundry in our bathtub, hung it out, and then took in the almost dry clothes and sheets to iron them. The idea of foregoing the ironing never dawned on me for several months. So I stood at the ironing board listening, crying. Then here and there I understood something; hilariously happy I would finish the ironing in a flash!

Typically enough, the words our children first learned in English were not the proper ones I wanted them to utter in social settings, like "thank you" or "please." Instead they learned "Schlitz, that's real beer." Our neighbors had a TV, and the often repeated advertisements were perfect for teaching language: pictures with sound.

ꙮ

In the middle of March, 1975, we arrived in Tübingen to visit a former colleague and his family who, during their stay at Harvard, had become our best friends. They picked us up in Stuttgart. We had not yet crammed into their car when we had the feeling that we were right back when we had been neighbors and their children felt just as much at home in our house as ours did at theirs. Hardly a day went by in those short two years without a mutual visit: morning coffee, sherry before dinner, or—most often—a late nightcap. Now we had come for the twins' confirmation, which was to take place the following day.

It was a bleak day, and the church—in spite of being very modern and in the round—was cold and austere. The pastor had asked the children to formulate and write down their own creed, and they now recited what they had written. Their creed was vague and general but specific enough to make me wonder whether it is fair to ask children to formulate their faith at their own confirmation. At one time, when the existence of God was as solid as this table, and everybody took that truth as demonstrated in rock, hills, rivers, and stars, as well as in history and current affairs—then it would have made sense to ask the children on the verge of adulthood what they believed. But then nobody did. Now that everything and everyone around us has been thoroughly removed from the sacred, to ask the young and insecure to formulate a creed is like asking them to build a rainbow. They have neither the knowledge, the experience, nor the maturity to approach such a task. Just as in baptism, they still live on our faith; we, the grown-ups, are still their godparents. It is up to us to help bring them up, not in the old slavish way with "repeat after me," but to help them live. The creed is such a cerebral thing that it takes years, a lifetime, really to understand why it has been formulated like that. Children need nourishment; one way to starve them is to give them only the creed. This is the misunderstanding of *sola fide*.

☙

People often asked us why we were not faithful to our native tongue. Everything came at us in English, and it would have been most artificial for us to begin to translate the happenings before we related them to each other. How do you take time to translate the missile crisis or the Watergate hearings or the deliberations of the Judiciary Committee over a President's impeachment?

The wonderful thing about learning a new language is the way one begins to live it. You hear a word and you guess what it means. All words cannot be looked up in the dictionary. You try it out and perhaps find out that it didn't work all that well. So you work with that word and keep it on the front burner for a while until it is ready to cool and to be stored away and used when needed.

It took years before we found enough ease and liberation from the literal to recast stories and make them humorous in an English version.

To say something in a language not one's own means to assert one's own personality. Not all of us are capable of doing so. Our courage sinks when people begin to look at us with expectant and inquisitive eyes; the tail part of our magnificently started discourse becomes short and often just dull translation because we have been frightened back into "the native." Eventually it works, though I am still scared to strike up a conversation in a social setting, fearing that the person I talk to is going to find it unrewarding or that I will be unable to understand the exact meaning of a question.

When I am alone and reading Swedish books or articles, I think in Swedish and begin to argue with the author in Swedish. I go down to the kitchen and make myself lunch in Swedish. When someone calls on me, I sometimes answer in Swedish because I am too involved to switch over. Isolation makes me incoherent both in Swedish and in English. I noticed that when I was teaching, the problem went away and my improvement was remarkable. Sentences arranged themselves and were finished off without effort. I took note of this, and I thought, "How wonderful! I have now mastered speaking." But after having lost the opportunity to teach and being forced to express ideas, develop themes, and describe historical processes, I fell back on my own inner shorthand which by now is totally my own. Krister understands it. When we are alone, we both use it, but when somebody joins us, I leave it to him. He is used to verbalizing our impressions.

Bilingualism has many sides: for people of the jet set, scholars, immigrant housewives, children of diplomats. Ask around and you will hear of the pluses and minuses. Depending on whom you talk to, you will hear how it feels *not* to belong fully to any one group.

Many Americans ask me why Swedish churches are so empty. I give them sociological reasons because in most cases I think they are the most valid: people don't go to church simply because it no longer is the thing to do the way it once was. Only a small minority has made a conscious choice either for or against the church; among these most have come out against. Very few would say, "I have struggled with this for years; I can no longer believe." Rather, they drift away. For instance, they move to a new community and then come to the conclusion that they are more comfortable without ties to the church so they don't look it up. They are freed from something about which they felt vaguely ashamed.

Sunday after Sunday the Swedish church celebrates in a stiff and almost nineteenth-century manner. Year after year the same slow hymns, the same solemn intonation of the liturgy, the same reading of texts, the same pretentious style of preaching, the same enormous gaps in the pews between people, and the gulf between people and minister. To go to church in Sweden was often an ordeal for one's soul: in boredom one had to manipulate one's spirit into activity, whether in browsing through the hymnbook, studying the paintings on the walls and windows, concentrating on one's own problems, or contemplating some mantra. And then coming from church one had to defend one's having been there to suspicious friends who thought, even if they didn't say it out loud, "You don't believe that stuff, do you?" It was a matter of two different languages. And no qualified interpreters.

Who knows how long I would have stood the subtle social pressure had I not come to the Lutheran Church in Cambridge, Massachusetts. Suddenly everything was new, although it was familiar. I heard the hymns, the texts, the prayers in a new way. Since I had to translate it all back and forth, the words came alive. The texts were just wonderful, dreadful, but full of life. Since I could not follow the sermons (it took me almost a year before I felt sure that I could follow), I had a great deal of time for contemplation, supported by the texts, the new colors, and by the throng of people. In short, there was a music in church which had been completely lost on me before. Of course it had been present in the Swedish churches, but I was—as most others were—deaf to it.

For a precious period in my life I was released from thinking how much I believed, how far I could participate, how long I could stretch my loyalty. I had the opportunity just to sit and take it all in. It was like reliving the world of my childhood in a new dimension. In the Old Testament lessons all the stories came back, but now they no longer came back as stories but as metaphors and archetypes, rich in implication by sheer economy of words. The Psalms, Job, the Wisdom of Solomon, and Ecclesiastes all excited me with their beauty of language and poignancy. The hymns made me giggle at times over the nineteenth-century piety. I had a wonderful time exploring and discovering this new world that had been mine all along but that I had been too timid, too ashamed to let myself enter.

When I finally reached the point where I could follow and respond to the sermon, I was again gratified; the minister himself was also developing. Every Sunday there was something that had clicked for him and that he made us hear and think about. His sermon was not a finished or polished work; rather it was a baby he entrusted to us to nourish. I began to look forward to going to church, because it meant a drawing together of my whole world, cleansed by divine light. It was thus that I found out that there is nothing in the world as potent, nothing as creative as the Word. Could that have happened without the change of language? Maybe, but it would almost have demanded a drastic experience, something earthshaking that called for my interpretation. This happened to me now slowly, like walking in the country in the early morning through the dew-drenched fields, cleaner and greener than ever, and filled with unexpected webs and signs of life.

My whole family participated in this discovery through language, but only Krister and I and our oldest son, John, were rooted enough in another tradition to experience the unexpected liberation.

Must we mean what we say? Yes, but so many times we use words to fill empty spaces. Words are no longer sacred. We use them in order to test each other's sensibilities. We play with them in order to break down the established order that annoys us. How sincere are we when we say that we *mean* them?

At one time the oath was used to strengthen the sincerity and veracity of what was said. And the curse was used to exorcise the evil order, the vicious spell, the stinking odor of foul reality. One way to measure how secularized both the United States and Sweden are is to take note of the degree to which the oath and the curse have lost their meaning. In court people put their hands on the Bible and swear that they will speak the truth and then they begin to lie. We saw during the Watergate trial how perjury no longer frightened people. They had even been encouraged to perjure themselves. The oath, calling for God as one's character witness, no longer has a numinous ring. The curse has become mere cussing.

Maybe here we have a small clue as to what has happened to our language in secularization. We have lost the feeling that we are responsible before God for what happens around us. God is not called on to help us, and the devil is not screamed at for interfering.

The devil was declared officially dead in Sweden by an important daily newspaper in 1911. Many people snickered at that caper. It is hard to judge whether the strong belief in man's inherent goodness, proclaimed by the liberals and preached by the Social Democrats, has not in the end severely damaged the feeling for the sanctity of life. Many reforms have been founded on that principle, and much good has been accomplished, thanks to that notion. But watered down as we now often encounter it, it seems devastatingly impotent.

The oath and the curse have been hollowed out. That means that the two poles between which language has been strung up have fallen down. It means little what you say when you crawl in the dust. In the United States, the pledge of allegiance to the flag is a secular replacement oath. "For God and country" often means just "for country." My country right or wrong—love it or leave it.

It may not yet have come to the point where people perjure themselves in order to obtain personal advantages, wealth, and property. But wealth has become so desirable and so out of reach for two-thirds of the population that one can very well imagine a future when malpractice suits, real-estate suits, inheritance suits will grow into monsters. Where do we get the strength to exorcise those monsters? Where lies the power to uphold the words of truth and curse the devil out of this legal miasma? How do we learn not to take the name of God in vain?

✺

The story of Babel is a great story worthy of all the meditation devoted to it over the ages. In our age, engineers and business people are slaving over the problem of getting the tower to function. A hundred years ago the British founded their empire and had it running smoothly for a while on coal. The miners and the stokers were the indispensable laborers although they never were allowed to think of themselves as that important. They knew though, and Harry Martinsson who got the Nobel Prize in 1974 was one of them after World War I. He told us about it in his earliest poems.

Now we Americans are trying our hand at empire-building and this time we have run it on oil, domestic and foreign. But we are running out. The building itself has already reached far beyond the clouds, and we, the ground workers, can only guess what they are planning up there. The word has come down that they are going ahead with nuclear reactors; and because of the scarcity of uranium they are now planning more breeder reactors to keep the machinery going. We are scared, but letters and numbers drip down upon us. Who are we to judge when the experts speak? We have, however, noticed that there are wider and wider cracks in the building between the schools of experts.

The real mumbo-jumbo of today is not the language of theologians and philosophers but the language of the scientists and technologists whom the engineers, bankers, business people employ, trust, and follow with the politicians always in tow. We have again reached the impasse of paradox.

❦

We must not take the name of the Lord in vain. Be careful. There is no one human organ designed for speech. Yet to speak and communicate by word is what makes us human and "a little lower than the angels." The power of words to recreate is given us in speech.

Not by accident does it say that God created the world by a word. To discover the religious ring around language is to be brought to the sources and find that they bring forth fresh water. I am not saying, "Read the Bible." For a long period of my life that did little more than create problems for me. It was through a drastic move which isolated me from a familiar culture that I was able to see, hear, feel, and smell the words I slowly translated to myself.

Homer, Pindar, the Greek tragedies and, of course, Plato are likewise forever fresh due to their religious over- and undertones, their relationship to the whole. I am not making a list but must write the name that always comes to mind when I think of the English language: Shakespeare. Where would Shakespeare be, had he not been deeply conscious of the tension between heaven and hell, the living versus the dead, the oath versus the curse, the hymn to life versus the dread of destruction? If the poles are not religiously anchored within us, we will be unable to fathom speech. But if they are, then the least articulated grunt as well as the most elaborate prose will gain meaning and start playing music on our sounding board.

One does not need to be a Christian nor a believer in a creed to admit the enormous power of allusions in our literary tradition and particularly of allusions to the Bible. A writer is one who puts words together; but when our small words are not enough and we want our discoveries to be seen as significant, we hunt for parallels; we find the archetype and use the quotation and—wow! There it is with power, the picture we share, lending us its suggestivity.

Images shape us. Books create worlds into which we can move. Right now we are hunting for worlds to counter the frightening one in which we live; we are seeking images that can protect us and guide us—images that can be held before us as mantras to be contemplated and internalized. Such images are gifts precious to our spirit.

For me such an image became powerful and lent its particular beauty to my imagination of what is holy—perhaps just because it did not come in book form and was not chiseled out by a word worker. It is the incredibly beautiful picture of the earth taken by one of the astronauts on the return trip to earth. There she swims in dark blue space, our mother, our home, a jewel, shimmering, yet soft. There we live and must live together.

Languages, traditions, religions, customs, costumes, color, creeds, and sex have separated humankind. Here we have a picture of how we belong together. An image to replace the mighty image of Man drawn by Leonardo da Vinci, which has served so long as a symbol for our conquering civilization and which, not incidentally, inspired the creation of the astronauts and cosmonauts: Man as his own measure drawn within circles, being the center and reaching out with strong arms and legs to the periphery, the emblem that gave courage to Renaissance Man, the model for explorers, inventors, and the hero of the humanists. The picture of Mother Earth humbles that image of Man and forces us into new languages of nourishment, care, and survival, things that we formerly took for granted. Who would have believed that man could dirty the ocean, pollute the air, and have it in his power to blow the sphere to pieces? Now we know. The new image is needed to help us dare step into an anti-world, dare say that what once was good is now evil, what once was attractive is now obscene, what once was mighty is now powerless. Our use of language, our tool for communication is already at work with this new vision. This is a blessing.

CHAPTER 3

Observe the Sabbath, to Keep It Holy

A friend of ours, a professor of philosophy, told us a story about how he and his colleagues had discussed the concept of leisure; they became so engrossed that they decided to form a committee for the continuation of their talks. The whole thing folded, however, because the members could never find time to meet!

We live our lives by our calendar. Every engagement is written down, lest we forget. The impact of the new encounter erases the memory of the one just before. Students come in, class after class, year after year. Faces blur; papers, exams and grades, are put into folders. Work. But to professors is given one advantage, one benefit that actually should be the right of all people: every seventh year a sabbatical leave, a whole year free from teaching, appointments, committees, and duties. A year at leisure to spend as they will.

The origin of the sabbatical year is biblical: man's concern for rest, the need for being taken out of production, lying fallow like fields and yielding harvests at random.

Summers of childhood, endless they were. How could two short months seem so interminable? Sabbaticals are not for children; they are always on sabbatical—open to whatever happens, to whatever comes along, never shutting out things or people, but taking in the world, adapting to it, growing with it, never threatened by time. Sabbaticals are for those who work and are overworked, for those who are so occupied that they don't see what they are doing.

I had been a bit apprehensive of this sabbatical year: being alone with Krister, first out on the moors of Nantucket, then on the plains of Uppland, day after day, week after week, just the two of us, stripped of appointments, of teaching, of juggling time, and without the distraction of traffic and the stimulation of lectures, movies, theaters, friends, children, and grandchildren. How would we fare?

Day after day went by and one just about like the other. The doors between our studies were closed, but frequently opened to report something just read which had to be communicated in order to find out how well it had been understood. Krister worked on his Commentary on Romans, and I wrote articles for a dictionary of European literature which involved a quantity of diverse reading. Fredrika Bremer was beginning to surface as the subject for a book, and Kierkegaard was receding—no longer interfering with everything I did. Were we bored with each other? Not in the least. These sabbatical work days gave us back to one another. I discovered the little traits, twitches, witticisms, and humor in Krister's manner of being that I had been too busy to enjoy, had taken for granted, and had even been annoyed with when I was too busy with things of my own.

The routine was interrupted only by the celebrations of Sundays and the festivities of Advent, Christmas, and the Epiphany. The year rolled along with its changes of season, the church year closely following; and as rain, snow, slush, mud, and darkness were much in evidence, so were light, longing, preparation, anticipation, and grace.

So many times I have heard the opinion expressed that Sundays are boring, Sundays are the most excruciatingly slow and deadly days. If only Sunday could be excluded from the week. Now that the free Saturday has become an institution in the Western world, what do we do with Sunday?

Personally, I never cease to appreciate Sunday—a day when we can be lazy with good conscience, when we have the time to scan *The New York Times, The New Yorker, Newsweek,* and all the miscellaneous reading matter that falls through the mail slot. When weather does not cooperate and Sunday is rainy, cold, and windy, then so much the better; we do not feel compelled to commune with nature through walks, rides, skiing, or swimming. Instead we can read, watch a game or play one, mend a skirt, knit a sweater, write a letter, listen to the radio, stare out of the window, or into the fire in the fireplace, or do absolutely nothing. Nobody in the world—not even we ourselves—has the right to accuse us of being lazy or of wasting time. Sundays are to be looked forward to because they are an oasis in the week when nothing happens, when one has time to enjoy. It is a day when we can sit around the dinner table for hours in broad daylight, enjoying food, drink, and company and having the luxury of taking a nap afterwards. Sundays are holidays, festive and slow, and they last from sundown to sundown. Already on Saturday night I have the feeling that Sunday has begun and something ought to be done to manifest the celebration. The feeling comes from early years when my brother and I were big enough to pull the big rake up the gravel walk from the gate posts to the porch, around the garden and back, leaving behind us a neat straight pattern. Then a bath and clean clothes and underwear ready on a chair to be put on before we were called to come for supper, which did not begin before we had listened to the church bells ringing vesper at 6 P.M. over the Swedish radio and a deep dramatic voice reading the text for the upcoming Sunday.

Sundays are a gift that many of us do not know how to handle, a gift handed down from the Jewish Sabbath. It is meant for our comfort, and comfort agrees with all but the crankiest of our species.

Every Friday when I look out of my window in Cambridge, I see Jewish students walking fast to be on time for the sunset worship and the six o'clock meal. And every Saturday I see them walking their Sabbath walk around the block; I think they know what it means to enjoy the Sabbath. The Hillel House has been our neighbor for almost the whole time we have been in America. So we know from observation that the Sabbath for the Jews is by no means gloomy and heavy with all its rules. We have rejoiced often on hearing their vigorous singing and marveled at their endurance, which we attribute to youth rather than common practice.

Jewish customs and Jewish worship were totally unfamiliar to us when we first arrived at Cambridge. Only after Vatican Council II, which sparked ecumenical imagination and the idea of sharing, did we begin to get some insight. Before then I had no idea how Passover was celebrated today. Up to that time I knew personally only a handful of Jews. I was never aware of any anti-Semitism on my part, although in ignorance I might have uttered terribly offensive statements. On arrival in America, it was my innocent ambition to meet "Negroes" and "Jews"—two kinds of people that I was curious about. My naïveté was tremendous. My curiosity was not satisfied at Harvard, however. In those days, in the mid-fifties, Harvard had no Black professors, and the few Jewish ones did not surface as such. I might add, incidentally, that there were no women professors either. It was in 1956, at the time of the Suez crisis and during a course I was teaching, that I discovered the Jewish students and their tremendous involvement in the future of Israel.

I made naïve overtures to Orthodox Jewish people to come and join us for dinner but was put off by their polite but firm attitude toward food, china, and silver; I gathered they did not want to have anything to do with stupid goys. Only during the sixties when a rabbi was appointed dean of students at the Divinity School—a wonderfully patient man—did I understand that these attitudes were not meant for our exclusion but for our education. As a matter of fact, the attitudes were not our concern—they were part of the covenant between God and the Jews—something for us to behold and respect. Two more wars in Israel have consolidated the bond between Jews and Gentiles in the West, because Israel is our doing. She is our pride and our guilt.

At Utmyrby there were no Sabbath walkers. As we looked out over the plains, we saw church spires, but driving up to any of these churches during the week in order to enter was for the most part a futile exercise; during the week the churches were closed. And to walk the roads was to put one's life in jeopardy, because Saturday was the time when the Swedes were on wheels, driving fast to their summer houses or "freetime houses," as they are called. At the time we left Sweden in 1954, only a small minority owned a second home, but by 1974 these houses had mushroomed in groves along the inlets of every lake, stream, and sea. Volvos and Saabs were parked on stony dirt roads deep in the forest. The people who, one generation ago, left the countryside were now back for weekend visits to the quiet changes in nature, to clean air, wet rubber boots, to splitting wood, harvesting vegetables, cooking, sewing, reading, playing, quarrelling, and watching TV.

On Sundays we had a choice of seven churches, all within a range of a ten-minute drive. Every one of them was beautiful, but the queen was Kungs-Husby which dates all the way back to the eleventh century. It acquired its present shape at the beginning of the eighteenth century when large windows were set into the north wall. The frescoes which cover the ceiling and narthex were executed by an anonymous painter who lived at the close of the fifteenth century and who here created his version of Biblia Pauperum. In the chancel are the symbols of the Evangelists and the four Church Fathers: Augustine and Gregory in the north, and Hieronymous and Ambrose in the south. Paintings of the Ascension and of the Pentecost miracle decorate the vaults, as well as one depicting Cain killing his brother Abel, and—in an interesting juxtaposition— the portrayal of a hunter and a hare. Further down the aisle, Delilah cuts Samson's hair, and the whale spews out Jonah. The half-naked Noah is covered up by his son Shem, while the other two brothers laugh at their druken father. Isaac carries his bundle of wood and is then meekly made ready for sacrifice, while Christ on the opposite panel resists temptation by the devil. On the capitals we recognized the prophets. On one column David is warned by Nathan, while on its counterpart, Mary Magdalene anoints the feet of Christ. Our eyes were surprised by a large flock of geese. They illustrate a popular medieval fable about the fox who dressed up as a monk and preached to the geese, but in the process, he gets carried away and bites one of them. He subsequently meets his punishment; he is hanged by the geese. In the narthex we found a wonderful painting of the devil who writes down all the gossip he hears in church on a large piece of brown leather.

The church owns five medieval crucifixes: one is placed on the altar which has the shape of a sarcophagus. In the chancel we admired the stone sculpture of the Madonna, brought to this place from Southern Germany in the mid-fourteenth century.

With all this to surround us, plus the music and the familiar but ever surprising texts, we felt wonderfully rich. Although there were only a dozen people assembled, the services were not depressing.

This community out here on the plains is small. What was once a densely populated agricultural region has become sparsely inhabited. Due to mechanization and the resulting decrease in employment opportunities, many moved away to the alluring cities. The few who stayed look with amusement at how the trend is now reversed.

City folk come begging for a tiny piece of land. Sociologically enlightened and freed from the burden of being considered backward, these country people are now proud. And when in church, they meet and greet each other with fondness. They have overcome. They know who they are. They sing with confidence and listen ruefully to the word of God. Sunday seemed to be Sunday again on the plains of Uppland.

In their midst, we were greeted with genuine cordiality; they took us in. We responded with admiration for what this region is attempting to do for itself. It is old Sweden and new Sweden in an intriguing combination.

Lying in the bathtub, I was struck with the thought that Sabbath leisure and ordinary leisure differ in the same way as taking baths differ from taking showers. When difficulties arise and you are not sure how to cope, then you take a bath in the hope that while luxuriously soaking in the calm, warm, and soapy waters, your thoughts will order themselves and a solution will turn up. A shower does not serve that purpose. You take a shower when exhausted from a tennis match, when you feel sweaty and in need of getting clean. Showers are efficient and stimulating. But you don't rest under the showerhead. In the bathtub you do. All your muscles loosen up and thoughts wander in a leisurely fashion until they fasten on a thread that spins toward a solution.

You don't take a bath merely to get clean. That is secondary. The first benefit is the relaxation and reorganization of thought. In Cambridge and at Utmyrby we had wonderful, huge bathtubs which came to my rescue many a time. And on Nantucket I was too often reminded of my frustration and anger when I discovered that the contractor who built our house and who had promised me a good-sized bathtub instead installed one of those low "bottomwetters" where chest and knees compete for the advantage of being under water. I howled at him that he had committed a crime, but he did not understand what I was talking about. Being a practical no-nonsense American, he had no sympathy for "bathtub living."

Our sabbatical year was planned to have a glorious end: the European tour. Krister and I had traveled together before, but always with one point of destination and most often by car, with children and suitcases but without much money. Often we stopped at the most inexpensive hotels and asked if by chance they had a double room for five. This time was different. We had purchased Eurail passes, permitting us to go first class and interrupting our journey whenever and wherever we fancied. In the middle of March we closed the doors to Utmyrby and solitude and began our life as luxury gypsies. We were going to meet the spring in Southern Europe and follow it up back home.

It was my first visit to many of the places. I was excited at what I was about to see. We each packed a suitcase with summer clothes and started out. Spring was nowhere in sight. It rained in Hamburg and snowed in Tübingen. We froze in Florence and shivered in Rome. We almost died in Naples where we had the crazy idea of climbing Vesuvius on foot. Greece finally gave us wonderful, velvety summer nights.

I wrote a diary during the hours of being rocked to and fro in railway compartments while crisscrossing Europe. We looked through the window, we slept and dozed, read and chatted.

Of course we went sightseeing; of course we saw museums. We were in Rome for Easter. In Athens, a week later, it was still Lent. Below is a passage from my diary:

"All that I now see and experience for the first time is somehow not at all for the first time. I have seen it before in books, in journals, and in the movies. It is all so familiar. The very reason for 'the tour' used to be to hit upon the unfamiliar. Modern communication systems have removed that experience. Hundreds of guides spell out to thousands of tourists what they already know, what they already have seen, and what they will quickly forget, because they are robbed of the thrill of meeting the unexpected. Like robots these groups enter and leave the museums, the restaurants, the plazas. All was taken in—in advance. Nothing seems to be out there worth remembering as special except the little personal twists: the museum that was closed that Tuesday, the guide who had a cold, the strike that fouled up the planned route. The experience of the truly great is diminished. No wonder that ever so often I thought: 'Isn't that much smaller than I had imagined?'

"The most memorable experience for us was to meet people,

colleagues, former students who took us into their homes and entertained us graciously. What they said, what they showed us, and what they thought gained further luster and poignancy when we also met them in the milieu of their home. When they took us around, the stones began to live.

"How far we are from Goethe and his 'italienische Reise,' how far from all those who made pilgrimages to Weimar to meet Goethe and to listen to the great man speak on eternal questions. Not that eternal questions are no longer with us; they are always with us, reformulated again and again. But it is as if we did not know about answers and therefore are unable to ask the question. We look, make annotations, and forget."

❦

Vacation and travel have become victims of consumerism. People spend heedlessly on what to wear, where to go, what to drink, what to eat, what to do, what to see. A huge industry has taken care of our spare time, hindering us from thinking and relaxing in the right way in order to come back refreshed, perhaps with a new view.

Our whole moral outlook depends on these truly free times, and we should not be deprived of them. People come back from vacations dead tired from the strain of tourism. Not a thing they have heard on these buses has taught them to reflect on how other people live and how we will survive. TV, radio, and films make feeble attempts to teach, but for the most part they too do tourism. And the ads interrupt at regular intervals, reminding us that we should get out and shop.

❦

For us, the greatest and loveliest result of the sabbatical year was that it gave us our lives back. In small measure that is what the Sunday service is supposed to do every week. It gives us back the week for judgment and forgiveness. The purpose of worship is not to hear a sermon, to sing a hymn or two. It is something much larger: to come in contact with the world as it is and as we want it to be. Both, and at the same time. That's why it looks so silly to an outsider and observer who objects to the seemingly easy transition, not knowing that it is not easy at all. It is an ongoing process. Sunday after Sunday after Sunday. It is not habit; it is discipline and discipleship. In one short hour to moan and to mourn and then to forget oneself and join with joy the others in a mock-up banquet reminding us of bread—hunger, wine—blood, life—death, and resurrection—the hope that defies despair. You don't do that in an hour—the hour becomes only a manifestation of what it takes a lifetime to realize.

✿

Sabbatical rest is not the same as dropping out. On the contrary, it means to take a step back and think and rethink one's position in the world. What enterprise is it that I am engaged in?

A sabbatical year ought not to be a privilege reserved merely for professors. Audacious students now call for a sabbatical year; more power to them if their intention is to return each seventh year. Because it is only when you have been active and responsible and others depend on you and you on them, and you are engaged in an enterprise which has you in its web, that a sabbatical year is a wonderful breather, a means to catch up with yourself and with what you are doing, to judge how good it is or how bad. Keep the Sabbath hallowed and make it a human right. Clean up the mess of vacation linked to tourism and restore the rhythm between work and rest.

✿

In one of Dorothy Sayer's books, Lord Peter Wimsey is a weekend guest and the author describes the lovely calm and feeling of deliverance that settles on those guests who have decided not to go to church when the churchgoers after much scuffling around are finally off and gone. I remember that feeling well from my childhood. I would sit in a corner with a book intently staring at its pages, sharply aware of all the movement around me, the search for gloves and eyeglasses and checking the supply of collection money. Now and then someone would come by my chair and ask, "Aren't you coming?" The feeling of guilt for not being a joiner and the feeling of relief when they finally were out of the house, and I was alone for a long, delicious hour and a half. I would jump out of the chair and start strolling around and stretch—just to rid my muscles of pent-up tension. The record player supplied background music, and I for one used to dance with abandon. I think my father is truthful when he says that we were never forced to go to church, but he did exert subtle pressure when he straightened his hat and said, "Well, good-bye for a while."

When our children were growing up, I remembered. But I had begun to think there was no way out of this dilemma, no way of avoiding the tension between those who did and those who didn't. And yet I knew more by then, namely that the hour I spent in church could not be replaced at any other time. An hour of leisure to listen to music, read a book, dance with abandon, indulge in the bathtub, dream in bed, walk in the woods, could take place at other times— especially on that blessed Saturday. But the hour spent in church is irreplaceable. When I now leave for church on Sunday morning and return an hour and a half later, I can hardly believe that such a short time has elapsed. What could I have done in that length of time? Read a little, think somewhat, listen to music, finish a review, prepare a meal, yes. But compared to the cosmic importance and personal engagement that have taken place in church—no, it cannot be compared. Church time is eternal.

CHAPTER 4

Honor Your Father and Your Mother

The sabbatical meant a confrontation with my aging parents. There they stood at the airport, erect, smartly dressed and their love shining away the wrinkles. They looked so good and it was so good to hug them. But already in the car with all our fast talking, the wrinkles came out as they strained to listen and to follow.

Back in my old room I had another look at my relationship to the parents whom I had admired, for whom I had been ashamed, and to whom I have written letters during all these years, and the reevaluation lasted all year.

From the diary, November 22, 1975:

"How I now regret that my letters over the last twenty years addressed to my parents and written with them before my inner eye, have had one thought in mind: They are not to be worried. They must feel our love and be cheered. Knowing how the smallest disappointment is made into a disaster, my mention of even the tiniest hint of nostalgia made into a mountainous homesickness, these letters have been labors of love—not records of truth. Our stress and uncertainty, our dismay and sometimes horror over our new country and our place in it could only be touched upon superficially. How deep it went, how it tore our innards was never said straight."

My parents visited us during the spring of '69, the year of the student upheavals. I wonder what they thought and what kind of picture they got. Seldom in my life have I been so tired. I had Krister, the school, the students, and the faculty on my mind constantly while I simultaneously worried for our youngest son who lay immobilized with both legs in casts after an automobile accident. Meanwhile I organized sightseeing trips for my parents to see historic New England with its picturesque villages, Marblehead, Salem, Rockport, and Sturbridge Village.

❦

When I turn off the light, I can hear now as then my parents softly talk to each other in the adjoining bedroom. I cannot hear what they say, but I know from all the years that the doors between their rooms stood ajar, that they read the papers with constant comments, and then they talked about each one of their children. Finally my mother read aloud until the book fell out of her hand. By then my father had already long been asleep.

They probably are talking about us now, but the difference from my youth is that I am no longer curious. It is like having the children talk. The worry is that they fall asleep and the wish that they may sleep well.

To be fifty years old and still have your parents alive and in reasonably good shape is perhaps extraordinary, although it is not uncommon nowadays. I wonder how others live with this fact. Personally, my parents have dominated my attitudes toward so much in life. I have fought their influence and their ideas, but I have always been stuck on a few facts about them: (a) they are my parents, and so much in them is also in me; (b) their unfailing love and concern for me; (c) by moving to America, I withdrew their grandchildren from their almost overwhelming capacity for interest—to feed and clothe and tell stories to them. Yet they have kept it up through letters, presents and visits; (d) because of their unending goodness, they are difficult to be truthful to; (e) they are now old and vulnerable. These are complicated facts and I am not very good at living with them. For one thing, my whole education tells me that our relationship should be different. They ought to be my friends to whom I could talk when I am sad or down, and vice versa. But no. They are my parents. They are Father and Mother, and if I as much as hint at being in trouble, they are willing to step in and correct it. Were I to show disgust with living in America, they would command me: "Come home!" That is the main solution to all problems. "Come home and everything will be all right. We'll be together."

But to be home and lie in this bed where I was once as a child and now to listen to them is to reverse the roles. They are now the children. Slowly, gracefully, innocently they have turned a page in our family album. They no longer occupy center stage as far as the pictures are concerned. "Come home" means to flip the pages backwards or to meditate on the empty pages ahead but not to live and act decisively in the present.

One of the memories from the sabbatical that will always stay with me is from Christmas night. Krister's mother and my parents had come out to Utmyrby to celebrate with us together with my sister and her husband. And in order to lodge everybody comfortably, we had given our bedroom to my parents, and Krister was going to share a bedroom with his mother. Early Christmas morning I lit a candle and softly opened the door to Krister's room. He woke up and together we looked at his ninety-year-old mother, white-haired and rosy, sleeping curved like a tiny child in the huge bed. She slept so soundly that we hesitated to wake her to come with us to the early Christmas service. When she did wake up, she said with amazement that she generally did not sleep except in her own bed but that here she had felt so comfortable and safe that she had slept all night. She lives in the present as in an almost transparent china bowl, preserving the memories of the past as graceful ornaments.

Not so my parents. They had worried about fire and listened to every creak in the old woodwork. Authority and responsibility—imaginary though they might be—were still with them.

Over the year I had many conversations with my father and though revealing, almost none of them satisfactory. We are both strong-willed, and I want my father to be the most lucid thinker, the most admirable dialectician, the man with a clear memory of how it was and what a decisive role he played. He wants me to be a smart daughter whose good deeds everybody sees and praises. We both get exhausted and disappointed in showing the other that this is not how it is. Father tires from too much talk and too many hypotheses. He who is used to executive action gets restless from debating and breaks off with, "Oh, yes, yes," patting my hand. I, who just adore gabbing, get irritated and light a cigarette which irritates him. I find myself unable to make him look seriously at the other side of an issue long enough really to consider its merits and perhaps change his mind.

Yet he needs someone to talk to. He is by no means finished with life. It has been so remarkable. He grew up on a poor small farm where his father, in order to increase his income, also worked as the local shoemaker. My father was the youngest of nine children and the apple of his mother's eye. She was convinced that he was special. He should be educated and become a minister. She seems to have harbored no doubt that he was one of the elect, and although all her other children were lost—either by death or emigration to America—she had this Benjamin singled out for the service of the Lord in the "old country." Through her encouragement and against terrible odds during the hunger years of World War I, my father received his education at Lund University and became a minister. His mother never lived to see him ordained; she had died four years earlier.

Having heard Father tell the story many times, I now asked him if he at any time had any doubts that maybe he should have done something else. For me as a listener it had always been such a straight line laid out by God through grandmother.

Perhaps because of my prodding, he began to write his memoirs, and suddenly they reveal a struggle that has never been evident before. So I continued prodding until my brother told me, "Leave him alone. He has done a great piece of work; let him now rest." This threw me into a spin. Are old people like children? Are we to decide over them? What does "leave them alone" mean? Isn't life one long unending quest? Should we stop before we are stopped? It may seem naïve, but I had really never asked these questions seriously; I have only begun to ask them and have by no means formulated an answer. I have been so protected in life that most of its real pain, which comes with loss, has not hit me. I know I am coming closer, and I am trying to prepare myself. But I have to know these people who are so dear.

In talking with my parents about years past, they seem so bright and remember so well. It is when they are asked to generalize that they hesitate and and blur. Their student days when they met and fell in love have crystalized into perhaps ten well-polished stories. When asked not just to string these gems on the thread but perhaps also tell something about the thread, such as what they wanted to get out of education or what they actually got out of all those lectures and all those languages and the books they must have read and accounted for, then they demur.

New knowledge and information is interesting, but it does not seem to make a dent in what seems to be a solid suit of armor in their way of life. I look at them as they sit drinking tea with biscuits, cheese, butter, marmalade, little cookies, and buns. On the table are candles, but in the corner stand radio, TV; in the garage the car, and overhead we hear the distant roar of a plane. When I think of the fact that they grew up before the advent of electricity, then I begin to fathom their tranquility. Every invention that they saw break through meant an improvement in their lives. That this has been completely reversed is an interesting and maybe scaring fact, but it is for them no more than "information." For me such information has sunk below even the conscious level. Every day I am conscious of what tears the human fabric apart, and I am scared down to the very marrow of my bones. As I take part in their evening tea parties, I try to draw comfort from them and from what they have learned. But they hedge on what to teach. They talk about blessings and divide the world into good and evil powers which are so blatantly simple and seem to have little to do with what we have to struggle with now. For them the United States is a good country because it came to the rescue during the two world wars. Roosevelt was good; Hilter was evil; Stalin was bad. If I then talk about the arms production and the arms sale and the imperialism of the United States, I make them very uncomfortable—because somehow the United States has to be on the side of the angels and Russia on the side of the devil. Although they know that Mao has done wonders for China, they don't want to register that fact. Neither do they want to wrestle with questions concerned with power, with different language levels, with paradoxes. Israel—where they went on pilgrimages—is a good country, because it was the country of the Lord. Israel is the country of the Bible, the Holy Land. All these opinions are plates in the armor; and after a period of bantering, my father says, "Yes, yes, my dear," and pats my hand. These issues which for me are a matter of survival are for him superfluous. The only issue that now can catch his interest and hold it for hours on end is when he and Krister discuss the New Testament and what St. Paul must have meant by such and such an utterance. That for him is not a matter of survival but a matter of salvation. He leans forward in the chair, pressing his fingertips together, supporting his chin between index and long finger, nodding, rocking slightly, then commenting and waiting for an answer, changing position and clutching his elbows with restless fingers. Absentmindedly he breaks a wafer, spreads it with plenty of butter, adds an ample slice of cheese and tops it off with the other part of the wafer. He then holds the whole creation over his teacup while he takes a healthy bite and the crumbs shower the brown surface. He drinks a swallow but has not missed a word. In fact, I do not think he has been aware of eating. It has been a way of increasing attention, a habit like smoking for me.

All the while my mother has been listening absentmindedly, although she puts on a face of intense interest. She looks from one to the other—her forehead furrowed and her mouth in motion. She enters the conversation only when a recollection is requested, and then she answers with another reminiscence. She has narrowed her sphere of interest to children and grandchildren and a small circle of friends and watches anxiously over the unfolding of their life stories. Mother is a natural for the soap opera, though she would not know what that term means. She used to be a *nämndeman* (judge) and thus got a strong bent for the tragicomical, although she would not define it in that manner. I hardly dare mention any disappointment or hardship because I know that will register and reinforce her sentimental views. She sees her role in life as a consoler. She embraces, kisses and cries, " How sad it is! But how nice that . . . "

Mother is the muse in Father's life. She was the "most beautiful coed" at the university, and he considered himself unbelievably lucky to win her hand. She was cheerful, whimsical, fun, and pious. Above all, she had an unshakeable belief in Father's great capacities. Since she had plenty of household help, she took an unending interest in his work, in the four children, and eventually in the grandchildren. Her ability to empathize, however, made her a difficult confidante; she identified too much and misinterpreted, thus creating more conflict instead of lessening tensions. Her optimism and lack of psychological insight, in combination with her imagination and good will, brought about the strangest situations. We, her children, receiving all her devotion and all her partiality, are grateful for that love; but only when we were in our late teens did we begin to realize that we were not living in the real world and that Mother was the integral cause of our estrangement. When we joined the rest of the world in being on guard, her optimistic bent took a sharp dive and she became exclusively pessimistic. With Father as her only remaining charge, she watches every sign of decline and sickness; and though she dreads them, they confirm her view of the total depravity of life. One can have lots of fun with Mother, but the gaiety does not last, the memory does not count. She feels safe with the view of "total depravity" and flees back to it and she welcomes every confirmation of this view.

My parents' voices from the bedroom are nevertheless the signs of a happy old couple, kidding each other while helping each other. People are, on the whole, much happier than they think they are, and my parents are luxuriously happy because they are truly grateful for their life together.

They know what is ahead of them. Mother dreads it, while Father seems resigned. As a matter of fact, had I not come along last year with my prodding, he would already have been in a world of sainthood. Gone was the powerful man of decision. The successor was the saintly man, full of love for the world he was going to leave, full of humor, good words, and good deeds for anyone that came his way—Mother trailing after him with admiration, spiced with anxiety. My challenge to him that he write his memoirs brought about conflict where he had already spread out a comforting coverlet. His wish had been to die in peace and at peace with everybody. A rose-colored, forgiving forgetfulness. I ripped that coverlet off by forcing him to remember, and, as a consequence, to suffer and feel guilty about incidents of the past. Time and time again he has said, "I have to write this out of me." When I looked at the result, I could not understand what it had been that had plagued him so in these seemingly innocent mistakes and temporary lapses of judgment.

Was I wrong? I turned my father around from a man having lived in hope to a man living in memory. Maybe my brother was far more charitable when he asked me to leave Father alone? One thing I know is that I returned him to life, to the tension that is the pulse of life. It made him unhappy, but it made him alive. These memoirs that I had envisioned would give him pleasure, also gave him intense pain. The past overshadowed the future, and in this perspective he again was in need of full absolution.

Maybe one of the reasons why the writing is painful for him is that Mother, who has been his faithful companion, has also been made by him into a faithful servant. He carries the weight of being responsible for her life. Since he now is living his life backwards, he understands so many things that previously he did not see nor heed while they were taking place.

One of the cruelest turns in life occurs just as a woman is through with childrearing (a procedure where she has existentially involved body, mind, and soul for often as long as thirty years if the children number more than two and are spaced out): when that glorious time arrives and the woman should be "on her own," she is also passée, fast approaching menopause. At the very time when she most needs work and other people around her to give her a feeling of her worth and her contributions, she is left alone with her self-doubts. Menopause literally means an end to the months. Not until modern times has the menopause begun to be considered a pause at mid-course. It used to be a time for women to die because they were worn out. The old-fashioned male chauvinist saying, "He went through three women in his lifetime," sounds gruesome, but it is true historically. The burden of childbearing and rearing wore women out. Modern women still remember that history in their own bodies. The ability to take charge of their bodies and their lives and to make the menopause into a purely biological fact mid-course is not supported by society—with job offers and appreciation of skills. It certainly could mean an enormous contribution to these women's peace of mind and feel of worth, if their skills could be salvaged.

Mother's withdrawal coincided with the menopause. And I think that Father now feels guilty and we, the children, feel guilty that we did not help and support her during that period when she ventured forth. We laughed at her judgeship, and kidded her about her women's clubs. Since all her duties were voluntary and had complications in tow, I can imagine how her self-doubt grew till the only place she felt safe was at home. That is where we and Father used to see her and loved to see her. And that is where this beautiful but insecure woman took refuge while her hair greyed, her body grew heavy, her eyes dimmed, her vivaciousness turned erratic, and pessimism overwhelmed her.

I can imagine how Father feels while he is sitting there penning his memoirs—where every move is shadowed by the person who was always there but never entered the action—this person whom he loves and who has let her life be completely molded by his actions. I can imagine, because as a daughter I feel badly that I never grew up to become my mother's friend, to share with her our troubles, and to force her out of herself and the very narrow world she has finally defined and kept to herself.

Mother had highflying dreams for all her four children; she also had care for her grandchildren. The whole period I studied at the university I knew that I could leave the children with her for as long as I needed a break—a day, a week, or a month. At one time she took care of Anna for five consecutive months while I was in France: meticulous and loving care for which I cannot thank her enough. And yet on my fiftieth birthday it was she who thanked me for letting her do it.

I took those grandchildren away from her and brought them up in the United States. I was very annoyed when I saw the deep effect our move had on Mother. I vowed right then and there that I would never get so enamored with having my children close by, nor would I resent it when they moved away. I would be so much more realistic and envision a future with my children spread over the globe. I would abandon all expectations of a close, near relationship. I tried to tell Mother that although we went far away, we would always be in touch. But that was scant consolation. I now understand this, because some of my favorite daydreams concern my own grandchildren!

Mother has had to let go of all her charges. It seems that we have taken pride in showing that we no longer needed her. Finally she has Father as the sole purpose of her life. He dares not die, because she is his responsibility; he knows her dependency and realizes that the one thing she wants in life is to be with him. She cannot die either, because that would be to leave him.

In 1972 they visited us for the last time. The flight nearly killed Father, whose heart disliked the long hours of sitting—legs down— in a cramped plane seat. They came for our daughter's wedding; at that joyous celebration they were just as much part as they were apart. Standing next to us, Father in a dark blue pinstriped suit, immaculate white shirt, and light grey silk tie, and Mother in a long light-blue silk dress, white shawl, long gloves, trying to follow the service. They looked beautiful, their faces radiating their love. But they also looked distinguished and European in a circle of people that had an unmistakably American appearance: a mixture of Catholics, Protestants, and Jews, white and Black, tuxedos and blue jeans. I was too busy and preoccupied at that time to participate from their point of view, to feel and follow their sentiment. I understand now how foreign it must have been and what a strain I put them under: this family is their family, yet so different, so unexpected, so mixed and so fragile. They were very tired after the wedding and that was not because of the strenuous flight.

By moving to America we have joined a completely different society—mobile and undistinguished. We are at home here because we have created a home—building on and modifying the model given us from home. The transitoriness of this society was plainly visible when my parents at the wedding stood in our midst, yet were in the periphery.

❦

Almost every time when we now meet there are efforts on their part to speak to me about what I think about life and death and life after death. I feel terribly sorry because that I cannot manage. I would just love to sit and listen to them, but they are waiting for an affirmation from me. They look just like children who have been corrected and rejected when I quickly change the subject. They are tired. Both are in their eighties, with physical ailments and diminished eyesight and hearing. They stretch their hands after me, they want to hold and be held. Since the sabbatical they have moved and now live comfortably in an apartment surrounded by other old people's apartments. Though they brought their most precious belongings, they are in a strange environment, stripped of the tangible signs of their former status. They managed the move, but with its enormous exhaustion they have little strength left to begin a different life. Energy comes in small spurts.

So now I sit with them in silence. I have often disappointed them by rushing ahead, planning for them, and forgetting something essential.

My young father taught me to play tennis. He beat me every time until I was eighteen. The last time we went to play is painful to recall. I had booked the court for me and a friend who stood me up. Father came home by chance and said he would play with me. Delighted, I rushed and changed, and we jumped into the car and took off. When we entered the court, my father asked, "Where are the balls?" In the excitement, I had forgotten them. He looked at me with such contempt and yet with so much love that I could have done anything—even steal—to get tennis balls. But he turned around and we drove home in silence. We never played again.

To see my old father standing on the sidewalk outside the Sheraton

Hotel in Stockholm, while I was sitting down next to a window in the bus to the airport did hurt so that I could hardly return his inquisitive, loving, and longing look. I knew that now we were going to be separated for more than a year, and that if I came back earlier, it would be to a funeral. The window was unbearably clean, and every wrinkle in his face creased when he tried to smile at me. I swallowed and grimaced and waved. I had tried and tried to make this departure just another goodbye, but he would have none of it. He wanted to accompany me to the terminal.

Honor your father and mother. In a Sunday-school manner I had thought that this commandment meant to obey our parents when we were little children. But that is, of course, not at all what it means. Neither does it mean to adopt their views and values which, by the way, all too many people do anyway after a small rebellious fling of opposition in their youth. It is our parents the commandment is concerned about and their welfare in old age. Will they be lonely, sick, hungry? Can they take care of themselves, or is it your duty to care for them—you who remember and can identify the events and the people they talk about and which they recollect more vividly with each passing year? Who but you can understand them when they helplessly sign their messages after a stroke or gasp for breath after a heart attack? When riding the bus out to the airport I felt so keenly that now the time had come for the reversal of roles. We have been focusing on the younger generation and its liberation from father and mother images, never letting these mighty figures diminish the way of nature, by aging and dying. We have concentrated on the necessity of each generation to get a chance to mature in its own way, but we have forgotten the bond within a family that is expressed in the commandment: Honor your father and mother.

I could have alienated myself from my parents had I not constantly been forced back to the basic fact that they gave me love. And though I went a different way from what they perhaps had hoped, they never rebuked me. I was the one who humiliated them by revealing the intellectually sloppy ideology they embraced and I chided them for their paternalistic relationship to people. I did not honor them for having taken care of themselves for so long and also for being the support of numerous friends and relatives. My parents have been fortunate people, but age is catching up. Their burden will increase, and I am far, far away. Boston—Stockholm—Boston: the trip costs about $700. That is how far my parents are from me. And then some, on which the price tag is missing.

Honor your father and your mother. That commandment has nothing to do with children obeying their parents. It means to recognize them in yourself. Marvel at the miracle that one plus one becomes oneself, which is a totally new being and yet so full of recognizable strains, habits, sayings, and gestures. The new creature grows up, becomes self-sufficient. The parents retire and become children anew. Honor them and you will live long in the land God has given you. I find this commandment most intriguing and most neglected today. Who says I have broken the Fourth Commandment? Well, I don't live in the land.

CHAPTER 5

You Shall Not Kill

Violence. What does all this massive dose of violence in movies or on TV tell us? Are we against it or not? Or do we accept that it is just there, and that it is within the human potential to commit violence, to dream about it, and to imagine it.

To be reasonable and tolerant was once the position of the powerful. Napoleon was not exiled once but twice. Neither tortured nor executed. But no more. A sort of madness has broken out in boils, as if it has been building up under the surface and has now come to a head. So let us at least confess that it exists. The United States has for a long time been arming its people, thinking that it was a good thing to be able to defend oneself. The one who defends himself with the deadliest weapons, however, is likely also to get killed in the process. Governments must now teach disarmament. For that they have no arguments, no verbal arsenal. A powerful lobby prevents them from learning how to speak out. Disarmament is our defense— that is a phrase that no politician has yet been ready to utter.

We, the American people, were party to murder in Indochina on a scale and in a manner that we still shy away from admitting. We now can admit that we had no business there. During this sabbatical year, our involvement in Vietnam finally came to an end and the propped-up government fell. But the actual killing of people, of social order, of cattle, of crops, and of hope has been so immense that the majority of our country does not want to think about it; people only satisfy themselves by saying, "Fifty thousand Americans were killed in this war and it was all a big mistake."

The commandment, "You shall not kill," is not fulfilled by our admission of having committed a mistake or an error in calculation. The commandment demands that we dig deeper into our human feelings and confess, "It was a sin for which we must repent or we will not be repaired and healed." Masochism? No, because if we refuse now to face up to what we did, we might, in our confusion, try it again, as we did—though covertly—in Chile. We begin congratulating ourselves on our success instead of acknowledging failure. We are in a murderous business!

Two photographs on the front page of the sabbatical year's newspaper come to mind: (1) Mr. Ford, one of the staunchest supporters of the Vietnam War, alights from a plane, smiling and clutching a Vietnamese baby; and (2) The Mayaguëz incident the morning after more than forty marines had been killed and untold numbers of Cambodians. Ford, Kissinger, and aides are pictured exhilarated and laughing, dressed in tuxedos. The big game plan had worked. We had demonstrated our will to fight.

We have heard many stories of Germans who long after World War II came up to the door of Danish, Norwegian, Dutch, or French people in once occupied territory, asking permission to show their wife and children around the house where they had lived during the war. We shrink with embarrassment when we hear of this insensitivity. But we are no better. Americans go cruising around the world. Our own feeling when in Athens was uncomfortable, since we were so conscious that it was the United States that had kept the Junta going. The liberation that was subsequently celebrated was not our doing. The Senate investigation of the CIA told that we were not involved directly in the Allende overthrow: "It was done entirely by Chileans." But who gave these Chileans the sense that they would succeed and would have the arms they needed?

We are now arming the world and encouraging people to use the arms for us—and coldly counting on the possibility that they may in the future be used against us. We are party to murder all right. Our taxes go in greatest measure for arms. In this country our legislation would indicate we care not about our children's education, but about their right to bear arms; not about their health, but about their right to purchase handguns without a license. This kind of talk, however, makes people very angry and most defensive. It is un-American. An immigrant talking this way might get the retort, "Love it or leave it."

Over the years I have had a few dreams which I have written down and which I remember only too well. They seemed worth recording because they reveal a repressed fear. It is the fear of death, annihiliation, and a guilt complex infesting our whole culture that not only survives but thrives on spreading and increasing the death threat. The dreams themselves show how complicated the issue is, and they are so woven into our braincells that danger signals are sent out at night, since no one has the time, the wits, or the courage to talk about it during the day. And what's more, who has the power to reverse our deadly course?

1958. The complacent days during the Eisenhower Administration were "pre-everything." Yet there were already race problems, unemployment, the arms race, and sale of arms, and United States' involvement in foreign governments. However, these were talked about but very little. New supermarkets mushroomed. Harvard Square began to look international. Route 128 (the ring around Boston) was building up with electronic companies. People were feeling that what they were doing was important and promoting progress. Gainfully employed. Yet in my dream I am walking down Green Street in Cambridge. It is dusk, which is rapidly changing into dark night. At first I walk in a leisurely way past small painted houses with flower gardens. The doors are closed with shiny brass doorknockers. No people are to be seen, but I know that here live white people. As night falls, the neighborhood changes: the houses look dilapidated, brown in color, and closer to the curb. The small gardens are overgrown with weeds and everywhere are baby carriages, big, unwieldy things, gaping, and empty outside the houses, waiting for the next occupancy. Wild roses stretch their thorny branches along the unpainted fences and onto the pavement, cracked by roots and harsh winters.

I am on my way to the hairdresser, and I am annoyed because I cannot remember that the street was ever that long. I am very late. The street is beginning to fill up with people who are all Black. The baby carriages get into motion—pushed by happy-looking mothers and followed by sad-looking fathers. I walk faster and faster, until I am stopped by the sound of an, "Oh," said in unison, a loud sigh, and then a long silence while all faces are upturned. The beautiful profiles—darkly discernible against the starlit sky— watch one star approaching with great speed. The moment is the most beautiful I could ever imagine because it is so awesome. I am alive with all my senses, unable to think, just able to watch, to feel the approach. Then comes the explosion. Soundless, enormous, like a giant fourth-of-July rocket. By the stark light, I see masses of people the moment before we are swept away. All standing motionless. Then darkness.

♦

In 1961, after the Cuban missile crisis, I was terribly upset with President Kennedy. I considered him a childish gambler who had no right to put the whole world in the pot and leave it up to the Russians to decide if we live or die. Krushchev became by hero because had had the strength to withdraw, the power to abstain from wielding power. This was not a popular stance and neither here nor in Russia could Krushchev live it down. This was, however, the greatest moment of his life and the reason why the whole world should be grateful to him. A power game had been encouraged. He had gone along. Now was the moment of truth—and he backed down. Will men like him ever rise to power again? Will women, who until recently have been obliged to negotiate from weakness, remember past skills and put survival before a show of strength? Will they remember that it is not only ourselves we are gambling with but the whole world—millions of people whose voice has never been raised nor heard, and whose votes have never been counted?

♦

In my dream I am sitting with my parents at home in the garden. I comment on how pleasant it is that they have cut down some old trees, so that you can now see all the way into the center of Stockholm where the sunlight is hitting the gold on the top of City Hall. (In reality this could never have happened. If they had chopped the place bare, all one would have been able to see would have been the neighbor's hilly lawn.) On the table is lemonade and cookies. My mother looks younger than usual. She wears a light blue dress which I remember from the thirties, and my father is in a dark pinstriped suit, though it is summer and warm in the air. I myself have on a red suit with a tight skirt and black highheeled shoes. For some reason the clothes were very much a part of the dream. We talk quietly while gazing over the city. I feel happy to be there for a visit, happy to be in my old home, happy to find the people, the city, the countryside so lovely, and the sun so beneficial and revealing only cleanliness, brightness, prosperity, and calm. Suddenly my father gives a start and his face shows utter horror. "No, no," he exclaims, and his head begins to shake. I look toward the horizon and I can't believe what I see. The steeple of the City Hall cracks neatly and falls silently. The Royal Palace breaks in two. The Riddarholm Church throws off its lacy spire. Closer to us the huge complexes of the two daily papers, *Svenska Dagbladet* and *Dagens Nyheter* split from top to bottom, and the graceful Traneberg Bridge folds and drops into Lake Mälar. The three of us jump to our feet. I scream and start running, but then stop to turn around, only to see my father sadly smile at me. He softly says to my mother, "Let us pray." My heel is caught in a crack of the terrace, and I fall quietly.

When I woke up from that dream, I remember I lingered in bed, nursing a rage. We all must die, but my parents are entitled to a grave, a funeral, a mourning period. Some maniacs far off cannot bomb to pieces a small neutral country with an indigenous culture, a people that has struggled for justice, democracy, and peace. They do not threaten, so why are they threatened?

In 1967—at the height of the Vietnam War—when no end was in sight, and President Johnson's "Great Society" was getting far too little attention, America was truly floundering, and the President's frustration obvious. Unemployment was down due to the war and the arms factories. Students were angry over the draft and tired of being analyzed. They demanded change instead. But we were hopelessly caught in Vietnam.

I dreamt that I was waiting in the car, sitting at the wheel. For some reason, our dog (who so often accompanied me on my trips to the airport or just to the grocery store) was now sitting in the back seat. I knew instantly that we were in Saigon, a city I had watched daily on television. We were standing still, and motorbikes and ordinary bicycles were passing us right and left. I heard firing but was not terribly upset. It was far off and sounded more like firecrackers. Looking down the streets, I could see the horizon ablaze in yellow and red. The dog whimpered. But suddenly the shooting came much closer. Magically all the people disappeared and the street was deserted. I was still just sitting as if watching a movie. The shooting was around every street corner. I looked to the left and to the right to see what might happen. Then something moved. A wounded man came limping out, clutching his gun. He stumbled and fell. Spontaneously, I opened the car door and called out to him. He saw me and began crawling toward the car. I motioned him to hurry up and to get into the car. Not until he was very close and I looked down into his face as I held the door open did the thought hit me, frightening me so that I woke up: "Is he one of ours or one of theirs?"

When I contemplated that dream the following morning, I began to sob uncontrollably. Never in my conscious hours had I ever divided Vietnam along "our" lines, nor thought of certain people there as "ours." But here in my dream, and quite logically so, "the enemy" turned up. To be sure we were on one side and would long continue to be remembered as belonging to that side. Vietnam as it is now will look upon us as the enemy which destroyed and ravaged its lovely country. Can we ever be forgiven? The scars on their faces and on ours, the white faces, the fear.

❦

The last dream that I want to record here occurred in 1972. The Vietnam War was still going on in spite of President Nixon's promise in 1968 that he would end the war. Just before the 1972 election, Mr. Kissinger had said that peace was at hand; during Christmas we had the heaviest bombing of North Vietnam ever. We celebrated Christmas in Sweden that year, and it was a great relief to be in a country that reacted swiftly with outrage when the news of the renewed bombings hit the headlines. There were spontaneous demonstrations. A handful of people started to march on the American Embassy. Christmas shoppers in the streets began to follow, clutching their bags. More and more people joined. This was something they felt they would rather do, something they ought to do. When they reached the Embassy, they numbered among the thousands. They had no clear idea what to say or do. Peacefully they just stood there, listened to some speeches, and then dispersed.

At that time I dreamt that I was out looking for someone, though I was not sure whom. More and more people seemed to be heading in the same direction and I followed. When we arrived at Stortorget, the big open square in the middle of the Old City of Stockholm, it became obvious that this was the center of action. People thronged in from all sides. Some kind of scaffolding had been erected in the center; but I did not pay too much attention, because I was out looking for one person in particular. I sneaked in and out, weaving my way through the crowd. Suddenly I caught sight of my sister-in-law whom I had not seen for years; I was so happy and I waved to her. Now it was summer and she had on a lovely summer dress. With her long, suntanned arms she motioned to me to come over. I reached her, but before we had a chance to embrace, she said with dark accusing eyes, "I never thought you would come. Now you must stay." In the next second the music began. A strange procession made its way to the scaffold, and in a panic I realized that I would be present at a beheading. A man in a long black gown read something which I could hear only partially, because I pleaded with my sister-in-law to go away with me. She sternly refused. Angrily and full of anticipatory fear I snorted, "I never thought you were Madame LaFarge." She did not deign to look at me but focused her whole attention on the man kneeling on the scaffold. Great commotion; I tried to find a way out. At that moment the man about to die turned his head slightly and looked right at me. He was so close that I could have touched him; his eyes were incredible, unforgettable, huge from fear, strong with accusation, shining with the desire to live. They came nearer and nearer. I woke up trembling, because I understood that he was I.

These four dreams all take place outdoors and in an urban setting. They are all pervaded by terror, and I admit were influenced by the movies, because they were beautifully arranged—in contrast to the horror of their content. They were political dreams, and they tell me how my unconscious has picked up the constant signals of destruction that beam from newspapers and TV.

Once upon a time people dreamt about hell and were afraid of going to hell. Now that a subterranean hell is removed from us, a very real submarine one has appeared. Poseidon and its equivalents silently scan the oceans, ready at any time to destroy human civilization. At night when only the clock counts the hours and the dark is filled with images, even Hieronymus Bosch appears lighthearted in comparison to the visions that rise between the bedposts.

Killing has become a kind of pastime in our century: World Wars I and II, Hiroshima, Nagasaki, Korea, Vietnam. The enormity of these atrocities is unfathomable. As sure as mathematics, they have created and doubled in us fear and revulsion which in turn create new horrors. To make us feel safe we have developed bigger and more and more means of destruction with potential beyond our imagination. But as we grow mute in awe of our creation, our internalization of the process is also in progress. How many mothers and fathers lying awake at night feel like standing up and screaming, "Stop the world, I want to get off." But since we are absolutely helpless, we also feel ridiculous in making empty gestures. So we remain in the dark counting the clock strike the hours, listening to the breathing of sleeping children. Maybe thinking, "This will come over us as a just punishment for what we have wrought."

But that cannot be. That would be just as foolish as to shudder and tremble before the prospect of going to hell and then putting a faint hope in a death-bed conversion. And as I lie wide awake at night, I wonder why it is that those of us whose fear pursues us into dreams and nightmares don't try to communicate with each other. Why don't we oppose this tyranny, this hell, by affirming the life we hope for and think it is our right to live? Why is the stench of death so strong around us? Why do terrorism, the torture and its unavoidable end, the mass killing so consume us that we cannot even whisper how lovely life is when people hold hands, share their bread and wine, give themselves up to each other?

When nations ask for aid from our country, what is it they get? Arms. What father—when asked by his children for a loaf of bread— gives them stones? What is then the result when the hungry have stones? They throw them back at the person who has bread but is unwilling to share. In the newspapers and on TV we see more and more often pictures of the hungry: the children with unnaturally huge eyes. We quickly turn the page or switch the channel. But at night the eyes are back to haunt us.

It is not my fault. He who is without sin cast the first stone. Sitting down at dinner with children and grandchildren, seeing their hands passing the dishes, loving their expressions, silently wishing them well, and hoping all the best for their future, sudden fear invades the heart, "What future?" The answer of the night must have a counterpart: the answer of the daylight of life and survival.

We are asked to participate in a game, a cruel game, because it pretends to be for the sake of our safety, our children's and our country's safety. To guard this safety huge submarines cruise day and night in eternal night. Sometimes they come fearfully close to one another. To insure our safety we now have enough TNT to kill every man, woman, and child fifty times over. Disarmament, which all of us ordinary people hope for and have eagerly listened and looked for for the last two decades, has been a game, a charade. Détente is merely a new game. We are the onlookers, not the participants. Were we really participants, we would be forced to take a stand, to reason in daylight, to let our killing instinct show for what it is and our instinct for survival be manifest.

We can reverse the trend by admitting humility before and exulting in the grandeur of life. Facing incredible odds people fight and conquer sickness and poverty. It all depends on our vision of a future.

❧

I would like to speak about a counterpoint dream that grew strong within me during our sabbatical stay at Utmyrby. It was not a night dream, but a daydream which became so vivid that when I looked around it almost became true.

Utmyrby is a small village consisting of four old farms, two of which are in operation today. The two others, with most of the land divided, have been bought by "summer people." Our friends own the middle big, red, old-fashioned farmhouse which they have lovingly restored and furnished with what they have inherited from their parents. The old furniture which must have looked odd in a city apartment has come home in this environment. Light from the surrounding plains is pouring in through the windows, lending colors to rag rugs, linen tablecloths, porcelain stoves, brass doorknobs, and heavy old bedspreads. You walk on wide floorboards, delighted with the clean space and the quiet rest that things alive with memories from another time and another way of life bring about. Our friends have cleverly and beautifully arranged the house in such a manner as to recall past times. Our friends' invitation to let us live there a less hurried but a more intimately involved life made me dream about having a similar house for my own family. My nesting instinct came to life with such a force that I could see this old new house of ours with my inner eye. I moved the furniture out of my parents' suburban villa and spaced it out in a country house. I invited parents, siblings, and nephews and nieces to come and to breathe, to congregate and to withdraw to the library with all the old books at their pleasure. My parents should not have to sell or give away their old belongings. In my dream house their furniture would be restored, revered, and used. At this place there should be no fear but that of nature itself, fear of storms, fire, floods, winter cold, and summer drought. And fear of human frailty: greed, pride, and envy. Here the generations would meet and learn from each other. Here they would work together. The mark of the place would be hospitality.

It was a love dream and Utmyrby encouraged the dream to the point that the thought became almost unbearable that it would never come true. I could see all of us around the large dining-room table, laughing at some memory of our childhood, correcting each other's recollections, while the next generation with ears wide open sat listening. I could find us at night in the living room: Father telling stories until the great-grandchildren were asked to go to bed, and Mother joining them after they had come in to say good night in their flannel pajamas and singing for them the innumerable songs and hymns she knows by heart. I could picture us outdoors on a summer day, working in the vegetable garden, or in the woodshed, proudly presenting the results. I could imagine the walk on Sunday to any one of the many neighboring churches and on arrival filling up a pew or two—singing loudly the hymns we so often practised during dishwashing or potato peeling. After church the moment in the church-yard, when we visited the dead and remembered the names and the faces, and then the quiet walk home to Sunday dinner.

So I daydreamed, seeing us come and go. No doubt Fredrika Bremer had a huge part in the creation of this idyl. Her novels concentrate on family life and family cares, seeing it from the perspective of the members of the collective and how they interact to promote or demote the status of the unit. It was truly a sabbatical dream. It gave courage and it increased my love for people—not merely my kin but for neighbors, real and imaginary ones, and for all people, because it taught me about the strength of the nesting instinct, the wish to tie together the past with the now in one place, the urge to issue a standing invitation to come and share as our friends had let us share.

❦

Night dreams and daydreams. They contrast but touch in reality. Let us talk more—much more—about our nightmares, of our share in the killing and in the threat of killing. And let us talk about our daydreams, about people we love and what we wish will happen to us all. Dreams seldom come true exactly but they make us happy or sad, inspire or dispirit. And the end of the dream is always the same. We wake up and we are alive.

You shall not kill. How can it be avoided if we secretly satisfy the killing instinct by not speaking out against weapons, against capital punishment? If we don't learn how to formulate living dreams? Each one of us is responsible for how we envision and shape the future.

CHAPTER 6

You Shall Not Commit Adultery

When people hear the word "sin," they usually think of the commandment, "You shall not commit adultery." For centuries that was *the* commandment which, if broken, tore big holes in the fabric of society. Although behavior patterns have changed greatly, we tend to cling to the old way of thinking and old-fashioned judgments. Artists may be given license, as they frequently are, but woe unto the public figure who breaks the official code. Witness for instance how the FBI, on orders from J. Edgar Hoover, tried to "get the dirt" on people. The surest way to smear someone like Martin Luther King was to dig up something about his sex life. Public persons—no matter what they do in private—must go on record as standing up for monogamy and must decry premarital sex, abortion, children out-of-wedlock, and divorce. Few will admit that the time is overdue to reevaluate this commandment and put it in line with the others. Thus, it is fair to ask whether Wilbur Mills committed far more dangerous acts against the people as Chairman of the Ways and Means Committee than he did when he was involved with a nightclub dancer.

Society has changed greatly in the last twenty years, but we are slow to admit the consequences. Why is that so? Because there are so many interconnected and intimate values at stake, and we are floundering. Thus, the family has been under heavy fire for more than two decades. Yet we are reluctant to see the significance of all the new findings for the structure of society. *Family* to our generation is still "sacred." For the majority of the world's population, family is the only social security. And we too have a deep-seated suspicion that we are kidding ourselves if we claim that what goes for the underdeveloped countries is not valid for us. Family is a source of security. When in doubt, people tend to hark back to the old and established.

ꙮ

Sex is a relationship, and as human beings we feel responsible for each other. Affectionately. If the relationship does not work, we

feel guilty. There is violent disappointment as well as great grati-
fication to be had in sexual relationship. A relationship severed,
hurts—no matter what relief it may give. One person is always hurt
more than the other. No one can measure the degree to which people
get involved. Human intimacy is a phenomenal gauge correcting
itself year after year, fine-tuning itself in sensitivity to the workings of
the relationship. Divorce is a descriptive word for parting.

❧

Sex belongs to our whole being. It is in fact the center thereof.
A castrated man or a raped woman does not feel that he or she has
been violated at only one part of the body (like losing a thumb or
an ear), but that they have been wronged as human beings. Sex is
an energy, a boiler, supplying the whole person, exciting or dis-
couraging us in whatever we do. It lets the imagination go to work.
When people say "mind and heart"—what they mean by "heart" is
a euphemism for this energy. A gut reaction. Obviously this energy
is at work in creative arts and also highly involved in a person's
religious life. When Freud said it was so, however, people drew the
wrong conclusions. Freud lived during the Victorian era when everything connected with sex was unmentionable in bourgeois circles.
Sex was considered low and beastly by the intellectuals of that time.
Freud's discovery that the "low" was connected with the "high"
terrified society. Religion came to be discredited and shamed by his
theory while sex was "liberalized." Thus secularized, sex has become
materialized and commercialized. The romantic yearnings and dreaming about "first love" have been wiped out, and fun and games have
been introduced.

During the sabbatical year, Krister and I for the first time in years
had time to be together in leisure, enjoying each other's company
without disturbance. It was different. Middle age had crept up on us;
we are middle-aged also in our sexual behavior. The eagerness of
youth that makes sexual intercourse almost a sport was a stage
long passed. We were not frantic about performance. But what we
learned that year was to play more. We had the time and the space
allowing sexual follow-up to a fanciful conversation, or just a sudden
gesture, or to common chores like brushing teeth or shoes, or peeling
potatoes. In short, we had the excitement of rediscovering each
other's company. This "togetherness" is of a private sort I cannot

describe or speak about but the years have made us fortunate, and the nuances are numerous thanks to our special education.

The central event that forged our "togetherness" was our emigration. Neither one of us can be sure whether we would have become friends the way we now are had we not left Sweden and come to a foreign country which forced us to check constantly with each other and listen to each other's impressions. So much seemed strange and different in subtle ways. Who was there to share experiences and inklings but the other? Emigration forced us to grow up, become friends, feel the alienation, enjoy our discoveries. Home became for us the other. If there was any known territory, it was here. Its familiarity was never boring but always reassuring. The world around us was full of surprise. And words go only so far. Every time we got together we did not know—and we still do not know—how it would work out. Marriage is a great gamble, and the process of education is long and capricious.

I had gone to a coeducational school. One by-product of coeducation was the ability it gave to see, feel, and sort out others' attractions and repulsions. When a flash of tenderness, a readiness to touch and embrace went like sudden brushfire through one's body and made everything glow, nothing was more marvelous than to discover that one was not alone in carrying the body's response to another person's behavior—that it was a reciprocal procedure. In school one could stand around, translating Latin, for instance, get stuck, start to joke about possible alternatives, and suddenly somebody would get silly and brilliant. One looked up and there was a glowing face, an awkward gesture, a wonderful, puzzled smile. In a rush through the body one knew what was going on. A smile acknowledging that one knew something. Nothing was said because what was there to say? The bell rang and the teacher started the lesson.

This form of recognizing each other's sexual impulses, their sudden rise from nowhere and their defusing in a smile, a begging off, became a way of socializing sex. Indeed it was a way of survival at a time when adolescent boys and girls were together from early morning to late afternoon. It was a way of taming the instinct, though nobody told us what we were doing. We learned through coeducation to recognize the source of imagination and its flows through mind and body. Later in life when two colleagues working together closely on some project felt this same attraction, they accepted it as something natural and knew how to handle it. The tragedy occurred when they did not take it for what it was, but called it "love," succumbed to it, nursed it along, and finally named it an "unavoidable Fate" that irresistibly had to break up their respective marriages.

In this country this mechanism is poorly understood. At the time of our arrival on these shores, I found out the hard way. A Swedish girl was for many synonymous with an easy "conquest." When, during our first years, my response to someone's advances was a smile of recognition (the beginning of a kind of understanding and fondness for one another, which in Sweden had often been the result), I here found myself pursued and fighting to get free. It caused anxiety that someone should think to have a claim to my person.

It startled me in retrospect to realize that I had always fallen in love with teachers. My father's strong image during my childhood must have played its part. My first love was our teacher in mathematics, a tall, then immensely tall (because I was only eleven), energetic man who was convinced that he could teach anyone mathematics. I did not listen to or grasp what he said or wrote on the blackboard, but I was spellbound by his vivacity paired with patience, his compassion for us, his slow-witted students.

My next great love was for the Latin teacher, a short (because now I was a full fifteen), unusually short though vigorous man, with an unending love for classical culture: Cicero, Horace, and Virgil. Though Latin was not at all the subject in which I would naturally have excelled, I wanted badly to do so and felt miserable that my capacity for concentration failed during the seemingly endless exercises in translation. But once he raised his head from the textbook and began pacing back and forth, telling us about ancient people—I lived for these fascinating moments. His ability to make me see and understand other ways of thinking and living drove me to elect Greek. Then I had it made. During the last two years of school I could sit in class for thirteen hours a week listening to this man's excursions into foreign landscapes. Particularly festive were the times when he read aloud to us, demonstrating an ability to reenact tragedy and comedy. The characters came alive; the issues were relevant; the plot, if tragic, made me wake up at night and, if comic, made me giggle at the dinner table where I made feeble attempts to emulate my teacher. I wanted to speak to him alone, to accompany him on his walks home, to carry his briefcase, to visit him, but of course I never did any of those things. Long after I left school for the university, I wrote to him but never dared send off my epistles.

How difficult and shocking it was for me when Krister in his sabbatical exuberance and leisure suggested that we make a sentimental journey, looking up all kinds of friends from our separate and joint youths. I wanted like him to rejoice in having the possibility to meet and relive old memories and share new experiences. Yet I knew that while he had walked a straight path—never fazed since he was a small boy—always being himself—I had wound the strangest course, trying and testing in greatest insecurity, often making a fool of myself. Meeting him had been a great revelation, because, for the first time, all my dreams, aspirations, and unformulated yet pressing questions found a counterpart with whom I could begin anew. Nothing in me had to be hidden or held back. The school years with all their unanswered questions and nebulous half-persons were just left behind.

During the last of those years I had had a boyfriend. He was older than I and went to another school. He was a wonderful person, imaginative, humorous, lively, warm, and inquisitive. I loved to learn from him and liked to be with him every day after school. He was till then the best thing that had ever happened to me. Yet I was so trained that I refused to dream the dreams of marriage with him; and when he brought it up, we split. But only for a short while. We were, after all, best friends and missed each other sorely. Soon we walked the four blocks that separated our homes. Again we kissed and laughed and cried together.

Together we learned the lessons of touch. With overwhelming emotion, the exhilarating joy over the recognition of reciprocity—when words bubble out as a mere accompaniment to the inward rush and then come to an abrupt stop. I remember moments, long sequences, when I lived so strongly in myself that I never even asked him what he felt. I was happy and I thought he must be too.

Long walks on crisp ice or snow, swimming in clear water, tickling each other with straws on a summer mountain, or splitting the streetlight reflected in puddles in darkest Fall—all accentuated by touch. Yet we never had sexual intercourse. I think if we had, it would have changed my entire life. It would have made me all absorbed. When I met Krister, I left him. What was ahead became the real thing. I dared not look back. I walked out of my early youth unresolved.

Now I braced myself and decided to face the past and at least admit to its ambiguities. I lifted the phone and called my former boyfriend, now married and living with his family in a small Swedish town. I told him we would be coming through and he invited us to dinner. We went and met wonderful people, but total strangers. Over the din of conversation I tried to recognize my own voice but found myself unable to. I liked these people very much. Their attitude toward life was reflected in their surroundings; their hospitality was immensely attractive. Had I never met him before I think we could have become friends.

My life's course has been my own, and led in its curious way to marriage. To deal with my unresolved youth, folded up behind me, now at the age of fifty, it somehow could not be opened and reexamined. It had been so intensely mine, and I had so neglected the thoughts and emotions of others that when it was over, all continuity was cut off.

❧

To have grown up in the pre-pill era makes it difficult to understand the children of today. We had sex education in school; it was presented on an elementary and rudimentary level. The idea of purchasing those devices the teacher had explained with objective, detached clarity never did occur to us—at least not to me. Sexual aspiration then was connected with what parents had told us about birds and bees, roses and brides, happiness, family, and the purpose of life. I personally was looking forward to marriage as a magnificent fulfillment of so many dreams that the little signs of potency demonstrated by classmates could in no way be related to, or compete with the larger concept. The idea of actually going to bed with one of them was not repugnant; it was absent—defused by some formless yet driving force. When that force in my later teens became explicitly erotic, it was already interwined with many strands of hopes for a future home, a career, a routine for daily life, and a dream of sharing ideas as well as beds. I made such an image for my marriage that when my boyfriend suggested that we might get married sometime in the future I felt he destroyed my dreams.

Sometimes I contemplate the possibility that had we been born just a decade later, I might not have fallen in love with the man who is now my husband. Since we were born in what I consider still to be the "age of innocence," I fell completely and absolutely in love with the most intelligent, articulate, witty, yet compassionate man I had ever met. Nor for a moment did I contemplate how he would be in bed. I had utter and absolute faith that it was going to be wonderful. I gave hardly a thought to the fact that he had trouble with a fused back, since I had only one wish: to be with him—all the time.

In retrospect I shudder when I think of what could have happened had I been more experienced and had less faith. I might have rejected him for the reason that he might not make a "good lover." Of that I knew nothing. We learned together.

Looking back, I am immensely grateful that I had no comparative memories to contend with, because married life was certainly a struggle. But not knowing the difference, we thought it wonderful. In retrospect, those first seven years were full of frustration; we did not know then that sex, like wine, had good years and not so good. We had all kinds of confusion but learned to admire and respect one another, thinking all the while that we had it very good, and being enormously grateful that it got better. Each night bound us closer together.

Jokingly, we used to say that the 1969 student rebellion ruined our sex life. Lying in bed, side by side, hardly saying a word, caressing each other soothingly, while our minds were on alternative choices to student demands. After all the shouting we now spoke softly about what could be the right move or the devastatingly wrong one. For the first time in our twenty-three-year-old marriage we faced a serious crisis where the responsibility was awesome and we became each other's escape-hatch. When we finally fell asleep, we did not sleep well, and always woke up around five o'clock, watching the dawn, waiting for the papers to arrive. For the first time in our married life we were involved not only in one another, meeting and getting joy from feeling out the movements. Hands just touched in tenderness. Drawn and void of spark, we scanned each other's eyes for smiles. When I watched the deepening lines in Krister's face, where flashes of anger shot red streaks up his neck, I too got angry on his behalf and was deeply worried. But at the same time I found solace and strength in touching his hands with the long, beautiful fingers. My whole body responded to his agony.

ॐ

Tenderness. There is a craving for tenderness, I think, for men and women alike. But strangely enough, sexual intercourse has become what hinders it the most in modern times. Since that ultimate expression of intimacy is so available without cost or risk, men do not train themselves to express tenderness in any other way. Women become afraid of eliciting tenderness—knowing that the slightest caress is considered an invitation. It is not less we want but more.

In the Bible it is recommended that newlyweds get a sabbatical year—which seems like a very good idea. On our sabbatical we had plenty of time. To smile, doing the same thing, hearing the same music; there was a natural coordination which is lacking in "normal" living. Having experienced that slow, extended routine, however, makes the "norm" so much more questionable.

For example, a husband comes home from an evening meeting. He is tired. He drinks a glass of bourbon, is happy to be away from all the complications, and at home with the person he knows, likes, and trusts; he wants to show and confirm that bond. So straight to bed. For a wife that often means to muster all the love there is in order to protect against the smell, to be able to follow the whirl-wind movements, and to respond to the silent urgent groping for her person. A trust and faith that the tenderness she craves will be the result of the intercourse, since it has no part in the overture. That the smile will break through afterwards and find response before sleep.

Modern life, with its stress and separate work tasks and different timetables, has greatly increased our need for tenderness, for "com-munity," as the students say. But many are sorely disappointed, because although the bedroom door is open, to go to bed is not always a solution.

Sex is a craving. There lurks danger and violence. At the last stage of sexual intercourse, one sometimes no longer knows what one is doing and does not care whether one lives or dies. Nothing is as frustrating as an intercourse gone awry. The pangs of disappointment make one want to hit something. And many people are hit and beaten, and many more are just hurt. In the center of their being they have been thwarted and, sadly, they carry their hurt out of the bedroom, compensating the feeling of inadequacy with the urge to succeed and dominate elsewhere. If this is done in the spirit of hatred and denial under the cloud of death, we are dealing with danger and destruction, because the spirit is vindictive.

To walk out of a murderous relationship is not adultery. What is it then? I have always been struck by the fluke of the word "adult" being stuck in there: a mature person unfaithful to that which brought him or her to maturity!

❦

Love and hate—so close to one another, following each other's movement. Sex can enhance the one as well as increase the other. How should we handle our sexual impulses, and how should we educate them to express what kind of person we are? On the success or disappointment of our sexual life depends our being with other people and also our covenant with God.

Kierkegaard had a love affair once which scared him when it came to the test. He had loved this girl, Regine, and in his imagination the two of them lived in a perfect marriage. But the moment he actually proposed and she was there in front of him as a living being, stunned, bewildered, and flattered, he understood that she was much more of a person and that their life together was perhaps to be more hers than his, and this he could not chance. The strong erotic attraction he felt had to be fought like the devil himself. The temptation to give himself up to her had to be rejected, because he had a task to accomplish, a god to serve; he would fail were he to give in to the temptation. Regine Olsen made Kierkegaard a poet, a religious poet serving a god who craved total dedication. Kierkegaard invested in absolute freedom from human ties in order to serve God in absolute submission. The God to whom he turned was the God of his father and of the church fathers (cf. St. Augustine), and the devil he fought was any sign of erotic attraction to women as an erosion of the image of God. He suffered tremendously from the conflict and his insight into suffering had its birth place in the severance.

Fredrika Bremer also feared that marriage would deprive her of her hard-won independence. Therefore she declined a proposal that very much intrigued her, because it came from her beloved teacher, Böklin. Her image of God was not the same as that of Kierkegaard. This was out of the question, since that image was male-colored and male-flavored and had shaped the very patriarchal society she was sure her God now wanted to change. When she chose to remain single, she meant that she was already ordained to be a servant of God—to do good deeds, to help, heal, redeem, give—to enable people to see God's goodness, to experience his ever unfolding wisdom in the creation of male and female together, because only together and as equals, as brothers and sisters, can they be fully human. Her letters exude fondness and comradeship for men and women alike. Her task and mission in life was to spread the good news that women, too, were the tools of God and that God had something very special in mind when he created men and women in his own image. This was the "promised land." She was another Moses, seeing that land as the future for humankind. Her message was that according to God's will the people should enter the land and work there together—with emphasis on *together.* Her model for living was the ideal family, a life form she rejected in order to be its prophet! A sentimental model, we say, yet we yearn for its tenderness.

The risk in the life of women of getting pregnant is, of course, the hard-core message of Women's Liberation: How can we remove these shackles and be liberated from the threat? At all times in history, there have been women who have chosen independence and individual freedom and who, through celibacy, have gained freedom of movement and have had a chance to use their creative powers according to their wish. But those women have been few in numbers.

What will power and celibacy could accomplish then can today be accomplished by the use of contraceptives and—yet greater will power. Western women have certainly gained liberation, but there is a loss of nerve to use it. Now that not just a few heroines are on hand, but a veritable army of them, there is little vision for the objectives of this war of liberation. It seems to me essential to guard the hard-won territory—to ascertain through medical research that the pills do not cause more harm than they prevent; to keep track of pharmaceutical production so that supplies are not dried up or priced out of sight for the ordinary person. In other words, never to take for granted the mechanical means, but always to remember that liberation is founded on a very narrow base. It would be to our shame if these decades of space were given and then women were wasted on goals that would not last if this base were to be removed. We should turn our imagination to ways of dealing with our freedom. Should it not, in the first place, be used to help and support and create a future for the children we now are able to accept gratefully? Instead of putting them away, as we also put away our elderly, should we not concentrate on the kind of society we wish for them? Women have not yet given guidance for the building of a new society. Instead, they are just participating in the disintegration of the old, taking the money and running. Women want day-care centers today—having their dependents taken care of nicely without being bothered and tied down. Old people sit and watch TV in the common room of an old people's home, and children dance "ring around the rosie" at a day-care center. Both feel terribly lonely because they have no part in society. Modern women have huge responsibilities which they have not begun to face.

Intimacy and partnership. Krister and I began our life together, taking these two fundamental concepts for granted. In Sweden we considered the battle for equality as nearly won. All through our married life our attitude has remained the same. But it was during the sabbatical year that I had time to reflect on how lop-sided the partnership had become in America, especially after the children had left home. Our sabbatical year restored the balance. We were together. We did the same things; we did different things; and I thrived because of the absence of inferiority. When we returned, my struggle against losing my maturity began anew; Krister was immediately absorbed by his work, while I was lost. That was a blow. And it was a blow that it was a blow.

To be creative, to be beautiful, each person needs independence, needs room to develop and flourish. But in suffering we need each other. Woe unto those who have never developed the ability to be with someone. They suffer the more. There is nothing beautiful about suffering. Nevertheless, it takes a great deal of time. It is not an accident that the marriage ritual reads, "for richer, for poorer, in sickness and in health." "For poorer" and "in sickness": in bad, sad times when we are down and out—that is when we need each other. We are ugly when we cry. To dare cry with someone is comfort. Nowadays, however, much lonely crying is done over unsuccessful relationships—which seems to me to indicate that there is a fundamental, romantic misunderstanding of what marriage means. It is not house and home, or even children, but it is to have a helpmeet "for richer, for poorer, in sickness and in health."

۞

As a child I read a story by Selma Lagerlöf that I have never reread. It told of a woman who had a recurring dream which revealed to her the change in her love for her husband. The first time she dreamt it, she saw a huge piece of purple cloth enveloping everything. But as time went by, it was as if scissors had gone to work; each time she dreamt about the cloth, it was trimmed off at the edges, getting smaller and smaller. She grew more and more fearful of her dream, and finally when the cloth was almost gone, *it* was her nightmare. I remember how sad I thought the story was then and how strong an impression it made. Because forty years later I came to think of it, and staring through the window, I thought I would try to visualize my love producing a counter-image to the purple cloth. I squinted, and the paradoxical picture of an upside-down tree presented itself.

My love is like a tree falling out of the sky; its roots are in the clouds or in heaven with God, if you will. They are hidden from me, but the trunk is not. The shape of the two sturdy branches pointing in different directions is distinct; I know them well, because when I was little I played like a satisfied squirrel with my sister and my brothers up and around, in and out, jumping without fear, from father to mother. But my love fell from that first original joint and for a while—several feet it was unproductive—just steadying itself, forming a tiny ring of offshoots, while the trunk was getting thick, falling deeper, joining my husband, and forming the crown that has three main branches, our children—each with its definite shape; and then come many smaller branches. Looking at my tree in summertime I see it is so thick, so surprisingly green with occasional leaves sprouting—all the people that visit and get in touch with us and enrich our lives. We have been very fortunate to have been able to attract and provide hospitality to many who have left us the richer. Looking at my tree now in autumn, I am amazed how colorful its foliage is. Anticipating what it will be in wintertime when I will discover where the tree has grown strong; through deadness and blackness and ice I will see how huge it has become, just sinking closer and closer to the ground. The day my parents die the tree will be severely tested, and only with the assistance of others can that wound be pruned and the scar blackened and confined.

If Krister dies, the tree will shake and split and be close to death. Perhaps it will be unable to grow any more, since my love does not grow out of will. The spring might be late in coming. The mightiest branches will be on the ground, and I will long to be there. The big crown—not feeling pride and joy—will be heavy, and many branches must die because my love is not strong enough. That is when the roots must help to supply new growth. That is when they will be tested.

One day the tree will touch the earth and disappear. The mysterious roots that were invisible, deep, and varied—what will happen to them? They are still in the clouds, in heaven with God, if you will. I cannot shield or protect my love. I can stop squinting and erase the picture of my tree. It makes no difference. I can only grow and wither with my love.

CHAPTER 7

You Shall Not Steal

It has been said that the twentieth century should be designated "the century of the child." And indeed it has been in the most blatantly superficial way. Never before has the child been so nourished and so studied—its adolescence taken seriously and its youth glorified. We have indulged in our children to make certain that their life would be better than ours. The future could be bigger and greater if he or she were but bold enough to conquer it. Expand and vindicate. Explore and exploit. Reach the summit. Compete and find the limits of your capacity. This is a healthy process. Health became a primary value. Health defined as youthful vigor. Vitamins galore were forcefed to unsuspecting kids who grew bigger and more restless than ever in a shrinking world—not in terms of distances but in terms of opportunities. A young person came to fear and distrust the old and aging. A young person could no longer dream of the future because all the facts about it were grim. A young person for whom youth itself was of value, since only during youth could one have a reasonable warranty of health, beauty, and freedom. A migrant generation that roamed the globe.

That all people have a right to health was not considered, since health was defined in narrow terms. Opportunity was not coupled with health. Very few people thought of fighting for laws to protect this right which seemed to be merely something given or something to be attained. All the feverish enterprises most often destroyed health, though they gained wealth for the strongest and the fittest in the competition.

Health cannot be measured in money. The pursuit of happiness should actually have more to do with health than with money. A happy person—according to convention—is someone looking young and fit and well-heeled. Clothes, dogs and cats, houses, boats and planes, jewels on unwrinkled skin, golf clubs, tennis rackets, skis and skates, summer and winter alike. An artificial health. There are very few healthy people in this world according to this standard, and it makes millions unhappy to think how "unhealthy" they are. To live happily will never be a reality for them.

We need a redefinition of health, which would be just as valid and correct in India as it is in the United States. Many, many young people growing up in the United States or in Northern Europe congratulate themselves that they were born, for instance, white Anglo-Saxon Protestants, because this heritage gives them a glorious headstart in life. They feel sorry for the huddled masses, and in liberal moments they want to lift them up to their standard. These young people ought to think about health.

Many businessmen are convinced that if the world understood efficiency and could employ excellent management, products and produce could be distributed all over the world. If only air conditioning were installed in hot and sticky climates, production and the living standard would go up. These people ought to think about health.

Many scientists project a better future if information centers were built and each community could be quickly computerized to obtain solutions to particular problems. The scientist on the spot would become a true medicine man of the future. These people ought to think about health.

There are many of us who grew up believing we were lucky, and in spite of wars, catastrophes, hunger, and poverty we held on to the vision of a glorious future because we had been spared. Now that our "immortal" generation is growing old, a rethinking and a groping for redefinitions is seriously beginning. What we have sown is becoming a threatening monster. We realize that we will not be here to tackle it when it attacks, but we know, too, that the tools for defense are not yet forged.

We cannot trust the young because they are created in our image. Though much quieter and with much less faith, they nevertheless continue on the path we staked. They envy us, even. They need our redefinitions to be able to stand the redistribution.

ψ

The wave of immigration that we were part of has facetiously been called the "brain drain." Scores of European intellectuals were invited to come here. Depending on their name and output they were offered professorships or lectureships, library facilities and bright students. There was a climate of sunshine and friendliness, of expansion and of getting down to brass-tacks work that was irresistible. Tolerance and loyalty were the hallmarks of the debates, and although participants in the university might have held different opinions, they always parted (or so it seemed) as friends bonded by a community style that characterized the university.

Harvard had been a Yankee place. Even when we arrived, its hegemony was Anglo-Saxon. It was still a local college, a small place, where people knew each other and had memories and stories to tell—understood in all their subtle overtones by the "in-group." Yet Harvard was driven by noble ambition to be not merely the best educational institution with the most Nobel laureates on its faculty, but also the most influential, the most crucial, the number one on all lists of winners.

A Harvard alumnus put enormous pride in his Alma Mater and would gladly sacrifice to enable the college to acquire yet another collection, another building, another center, or to buy another "name." Harvard's sprawling empire began to take shape. The center was in Cambridge, Mass., but the tentacles reached far: Washington D.C., New York, France, Italy, Greece, Iran, India, and Japan. The Harvard Business School expanded greatly; to have gone there was probably the best credential you could carry in your portfolio. Henry Kissinger began to run his seminars in international relations.

At the center all this was sweet innocence and fun. Who would not much rather be here where the action was? It seemed that in almost every field Harvard was excelling. Those were the fifties.

Then came the sixties and the question, "Who suffers when you excel?" began to creep up in seminars and lectures. The city of Cambridge that had always turned a slightly jaundiced eye toward Harvard began to groan audibly under the combined weight of the Harvard-M.I.T. expansions. Still there were no tenured women nor Blacks, and the list of professors' names still had a distinct Anglo-Saxon flavor. The unfavored groups became visible. Harvard was adjusting slowly in an orderly manner, it thought, when suddenly the rebellion broke out in the Spring of 1969. People said it couldn't happen at Harvard; it would not have happened at Harvard had not the Vietnam War so clearly indicated Harvard's involvement. The students lived under the threat of being drafted to participate in an undeclared war brought about by Harvard men. Harvard no longer meant to the students what it had meant to their fathers:

pride and excellence. It now meant exploitation and arrogance. "The best and the brightest" was all irony.

In 1956, when our oldest child reached the "year of the Indians" in school, we had a great crisis: the TV presented one side of the picture, the cowboy-Indian duel, while in school he learned about the intrusion of the pioneers on Indian territory—the nomad versus the settler—where the settler always won in the end. Our son learned about the breakdown of Indian customs, the feeling of superiority over the Indian religion, the destruction of Indian industry, and the introduction of alcohol that broke the will of Indian men. He learned about the miserable conditions in the Indian reservations and how the Indians were repeatedly cheated out of good land. He lectured us in front of the TV screen.

It comes as no surprise to me therefore that we are now getting Indian revolt and demands. Remembering the education of our children—how thoroughly and compassionately it dealt with the Indian plight—it had to bear fruit. The children were not just playing Cowboys and Indians in war games; they were taught to live the lives of the Indian people, and they learned to see things from the non-white side.

This has been a lesson for all of us in the mid-twentieth century. We have finally begun to understand the other side and to see ourselves as others see us—not a pretty picture.

I do not see the student revolution as the beginning of something new but rather as the end of an era—a reaction rather than an action. It was the result of all the questions that had been nagging us during the sixties—questions that perhaps can be summarized with "Where will it all end?" The Great Society had become a rolling juggernaut, crushing other people's cultures and the future of its own youth. Justice was slipping away, disappearing in the gap between rich and poor. Paradoxes were appearing everywhere. I will not say that the world has become better since 1969, but enormous changes have taken place. Maybe, in retrospect, we can even say that we were lucky to have had the experience of the student revolution because it did open the eyes of many who before had steadfastly refused to see that we were on a collision course.

❦

At the very end of our sabbatical year, Krister took part in an international and interfaith peace colloquium at Bellagio, Italy, where the topic for discussion was "The Energy/Food Crisis: A Challenge to Peace, A Call to Faith." Buddhists, Christians, Hindus, Jews, and Muslims met for five days in fellowship and prayer to appraise our common situation. On May 31, 1975, they issued the following statement:

> We met, conscious of the four hundred million—one-tenth of the world population—who lack sufficient food, one half of that number being children; a world of starvation and malnutrition causing permanent damage to brain and life; a world where many of the attempts at rectifying this situation have not worked but rather tended to make the rich richer and the poor poorer; a world which may double its population from the present four billion to eight billion prior to the year 2020.
>
> Under different symbols—powerful in our various traditions—there emerged a common vision in which "bread" and "rice" are far more than a commodity manipulated by the laws of market and commerce. The right to breathe the air and to drink the water becomes coupled with the right to eat. Some would even speak of the holiness of bread. To others, the basic human need for food leads to similar reverence for the fruits of the earth. In short, food is not just a commercial commodity among commodities, and cannot be so treated by society. And an enhanced dignity of the farmer must consequently be translated into improved economic status for him and for his almost sacred service to us all.
>
> We were made aware of how the scarcity of food and the scarcity of energy are closely related, and we became convinced that the first claim on resources of energy should be made for agricultural development in terms of fertilizers and irrigation, and that at a price acceptable to the less developed countries.
>
> We rejoiced in the efforts now getting underway through the World Food Council of the United Nations, grateful that this amount of cooperation between sovereign nations has been possible. We appreciate its emphasis on local development where it is most needed and promises more lasting effects. We hope reserves of grain will be so located that they can reach people in need speedily and efficiently.
>
> We were strengthened in our convictions that neither short-term nor long-term alleviation of hunger and malnutrition can be achieved without structural changes in the societies of which we are a part. In a world of scarcity, the increased affluence of the affluent is intolerable.

And it is unacceptable for the economic burden of a slowdown in the increasing standard of living in the affluent nations to be borne by the unemployed and the poor in those countries. Scarcity calls for a just distribution of resources, both within and among nations. In developing countries no less than in the developed ones, the first and last aim must be that of just distribution.

As religious communities and individuals we consider it our immediate duty to hold up this simple truth before ourselves and our political leaders, and for leaders of industry and finance, so that the poor may be assured their right to eat. We shall do so through organizations available to us and through local and national "food councils," working in cooperation with whatever agencies are formed to administer the programs of the World Food Council of the United Nations.

The deepest and strongest expression of any religion is the "style of life" that characterizes its believers. It is urgent that religious communities and individuals scrutinize their life style and turn from habits of waste, overconsumption and thoughtless acceptance of the standards propagated by advertisements and social pressures.

The cry from millions for food brought us together from many faiths. God—Reality itself—calls us to respond to the cry for food. And we hear it as a cry not only for aid but also for justice. The spirit—if not the words—of one of the prayers used in our meeting sums up not only our hope but our resolve: "Give bread to those who have hunger, and to those who have bread, give a hunger for justice."

This prayer has become our grace at the table, and when we look at the food we are about to eat, we are constantly reminded of our dilemma. We marvel at the riches of the world and wonder about the distribution. The statement indicates to me that something really new has happened. The global view is finally reality. The era of Columbus is dead. There are no undiscovered islands; we know our resources and we have to ration them, to share. The commandment stands, You shall not steal.

Behind us is the era of colonialism, of exploitation, and stealing in innocence. If that course were to be continued, it will no more be in ignorance but in cold blood. The future is not bright, but it is much more hopeful than the recent past. We must face the challenge to share, and that will require all our ingenuity. The world has seen manna come down from heaven and other bread miracles. Our real enemy is our greed.

John Maynard Keynes once wrote, tongue in cheek, that "capitalism is the extraordinary belief that the nastiest of men for the nastiest of motives will somehow work for the benefit of us all." I do not believe that human beings out of their own good will are going to share what they have fought hard to obtain. They are able to construe any kind of defense system. We therefore must build a system of sharing into a democratic order on which people can vote, with laws to which they can adhere. America is well equipped to achieve such a system because of her long tradition of generosity, but only if she is willing to look away from the days of conquest and look to the future with maturity and humility; she has seen from experience what inequality has wrought. It is high time to say "Goodbye Columbus," with the memory of what that period brought in terms of slavery, sickness, murder, and maiming.

∙❦∙

America is a true children's paradise. A toy, a snack, a dream-machine like TV, encouraging teachers, and doting parents are normal, taken for granted. Friends take interest in the children's upbringing, listen to them, and help them along. The way Americans live in one-family houses gives the children space. The way Americans take time with children enables them to articulate. We were astonished right from the start by the generous attention given our children from Krister's colleagues, from our landlords, from the wife of the president of Harvard, and from students who came to babysit.

Had we not come here, I am almost sure that we would never have thought that we could or should adopt a child. But in this country there was nothing extraordinary about it. A rather common phenomenon, we learned. Thus, when a letter arrived from Sweden asking us for money to support a baby boy who had just become an orphan, we talked about adopting him. True, we had no money, but we did have space—seven rooms and two big halls. We had a family and we were aglow with all the generosity that we had encountered. We could manage with a little help from our friends. So we went ahead. Thus we received a present from Sweden which has meant more to our family life than anything else. It complicated all our lives and thereby enriched them. And everybody supported us, friends, church, schools, doctors and—not the least important—the immigration office which made the mistake from the photo we sent in to mark his alien card with an "F" due to his long blond hair.

We sent it back for correction but found it on return still stamped with an F, signifying female. Krister, who thinks that the best way to deal with officialdom and bureaucracy is to write a distinct and personal letter, then wrote: "It might not be obvious to you as it is to us each night when we wash him in the bathtub that he is a male." This time the card was returned correctly marked and from then on, whenever I had occasion to visit the immigration office in Boston, they would smile and say, "Oh yes, Mrs. Stendahl, and how is the *boy*?"

❦

"Cast your bread upon the water" is an expression from the Bible often quoted in America, but practically unknown in Sweden. Swedes are institutionally extremely generous but individually cautious. In America the opposite is true. Both sides may have some negative effects. But the positive generosity as a phenomenon always surprises, gladdens, and makes people adventurous.

When our parents grew up, all they saw was progress; they marvelled at the new things their children could experience: travel, telephone, TV, airplanes. It was not so long before that the idea of flying had been laughed at. Now it is taken for granted. Nobody goes to Europe by ship any more. Nobody writes letters. Nobody carries water from the well. Nobody washes their clothes in the stream. We have been given an easier way.

On the other hand we know that it is going to be more difficult for our children and grandchildren in turn. For a long time people denied this, saying "That is their problem." But with the command-ments before our eyes, we know that we are cheating them. We are using up resources that cannot be replenished. We lie to them most seriously by flying about, flashing credit cards, accumulating things. We are settling them with an intolerable burden.

In 1948, looking at my tiny baby son, I knew that his upbringing could not be as rich as ours had been in terms of space and time. I regretted the loss of the closeness of family, the greatness of nature, the leisure of evenings, the freedom of walking alone at night, and above all the belief in a better future. Our three children were born in the atomic age.

The car, the telephone, and the TV represent many conveniences, but they also bring constant change and force the mind to adjust to calamity. Where once the burning down of a neighbor's house was an earthshaking catastrophe, we now hear bad news every night and are hardened to fires, robberies, kidnappings, murders. We are cheated out of a sense of proportion in life.

Children. I have been to the theater—an average performance—but for the first time I understood the universal problem in Chekhov's *Three Sisters.* Parents educate their children and heighten their expectations. The three sisters want things, they want a life-style that they can never get with their limited means. They are stuck in their petty bourgeois occupations, with wear and tear, and they never appreciate the joys available because those are always "beneath" them.

We got to Moscow. But will our children? Will our life-style be their hopeless dream?

CHAPTER 8

You Shall Not Bear False Witness Against Your Neighbor

The last seven commandments are really concerned about one's neighbors and not so much about one's own soul searching and the piling up of guilt upon guilt. Our way of living with one another is important; therefore our corporate life is just as crucial as the cross-examination of our hearts for secret desires not known or fully understood by us.

The Eighth Commandment does not say, "You shall not lie," but "You shall not bear false witness against your neighbor." When we stop to think about that, we realize its significance. The one occasion when it is of utmost importance that we speak the truth and nothing but the truth is when our neighbor is in trouble with the law and we are called upon to witness.

We have of late become intensely interested in personal truth as a result of the fascinating discovery of our ability to deceive ourselves. In that hot pursuit we often disregard others. Our own "guilt pile" has a tendency to rise so high that it screens from view our communal, ethnic, and national handling of the truth. Our collective falsehood might be quite sizeable.

At the long, yellow tables of *Carolina*, the university library in Uppsala, I once sat and pondered Ibsen's idea of the life-lie. In 1960, I wrote a paper on Ibsen's *Rosmersholm*. Back now in the remodeled library, with its leather chairs and round tables, I remembered the old paper. The pain brought by the effort to express what I wanted to say returned. In *The Wild Duck*, Ibsen in an admirable way manages to convey how all the characters bear the burden of a concealed lie. At the center is Hjalmar, incarnating the lie, one could say. He has always turned away from the truth and its unpleasantness, preferring to live a life of dreams that may or may not come true. Gina, his wife, prefers to support this attitude, because it makes life tolerable. She knows the truth, but she also knows that the truth is unacceptable to society. Gregers does not know the truth but lives with a passion for literal truth. He becomes a bloodhound, tracking it down—which leads to the death of the innocent daughter, Hedvig, whose birth was the origin of all the lying. *The Wild Duck* is clear and unequivocal.

Rosmersholm, on the other hand, is more tricky because there is not an act in the past that has been concealed and whose consequences we witness in the play. Instead we are dealing with the consequences of ideas and ideals which can be just as deadly even when they are embraced by otherwise powerless people. To understand this one must have been exposed to equivocal ideas and have shivered before the possibilities of their truth or falsehood.

In 1960, while sitting at the yellow table and surrounded by books on Ibsen, a legion of them, trying to keep them neatly together so they would not spill into the next student's territory, and gazing out of the large, tall windows up into the crowns of giant trees, I was not able to sort this out. The personal lie I could understand. That Hedvig was not the daughter of Hjalmar seemed to me enough of a basis for a drama dealing with the life-lie. I searched for a similar personal lie in Rosmer and thought that it might have been the femininity and dreaminess of his character that was his flaw. This extraordinary trait attracted and repulsed and drove ordinary people crazy. So I thought then. I did not take Rebecca's radical liberalism into account. A faith that made her act. To be a liberal, then, meant for me to be an observer and a critic. But Rosmer understands his part in strengthening her faith, giving her courage to act and therefore accepts a share in the guilt that drives her to suicide. The double suicide which seemed such a melodramatic ending, and most unfortunate from an aesthetic point of view, I now understand and I realize how Ibsen was on to the real thing.

During our first sabbatical in 1959–1960, we rented a small flat on the outski::ts of Uppsala at a pleasantly curved dirt road edged with low apartment houses with playgrounds and plenty of trees between them. The settlement was new and had been carefully laid out by city planners. In those days Sweden still had a housing shortage; the inhabitants were therefore a mixture of town and gown, workers, academicians, blue- and white-collar people. It was far from a "neighborhood" in the American sense. Yet it was a very peaceful, nice place to live. Each family unit led its own private life. No mixing socially. Nobody borrowed sugar.

One winter night with moonlight over the snow-clad ground, I was walking home rather slowly, peeking into apartment after apartment. Dinner was out of the way. Families were sitting around the kitchen or the living-room tables; children were doing homework; grown-ups were reading the paper or mending something. Brightly colored curtains, good lighting fixtures, well designed furniture, good quality kitchen equipment. In house after house the same. Being outside, I could not hear what they said, but they moved so softly or hardly at all. It was as if the whole street were waiting for something. As I saw this, I said to myself, "What will happen now in Sweden?" There is a reasonable security for all. There is mobility; the street was lined with cars bumper to bumper. There is health, quality, and cleanliness. What next?

Fourteen years later I walked down the same street. Cars were now of a later model; they had been driven off the street and were standing side by side in parking lots. Street lights were bright. But no longer could I see into the living rooms. They were all dark and emanated a yellow-greenish light. The country was glued to the tube.

ᴥ

When I was a child I made up my world from the stories my mother read or told to me. It never occurred to me to check them out with the real world. I had everything. I was a princess in a garden with all things at my disposal. I did not notice that there were knife-sharp borders until I was pushed by schoolmates against the fundamental shibboleth: God does not exist and Jesus never lived. My most beloved classmate told me so. First I thought it utterly ridiculous. Father, Mother, our home, and friends were completely enveloped by God. Days began and ended with prayer; at every meal we said "thank you" to God. In God we lived and had our being. Were we living a lie?

It seemed to me that the world was rent in two: on one side were my parents, and on the other—where God did not exist—were most of my classmates, teachers, and most writers and journalists. These nonbelievers never even considered the possibility of God. As I observed them, they were honest, humorous, fun to be around, helpful, but void of what I considered religion—a yielding before a greater power, a marvel before the miraculous.

The sun that stood still in the valley of Ajalon, the bush that burned without being consumed before Moses, the snake that had

entered paradise, the fire that struck Elijah's altar—all those wonderful stories that I had heard at my mother's knee—were they to be
thrown out with Cinderella's fairy godmother, Santa Claus, and the
wolf in Little Red Riding Hood? It seemed to me that this was
exactly what my peers had done gladly, while I was still full of
wonder. I could not sort it out. I could not translate myself into
their reality. I thought of myself as the only one in the class in
need of forgiveness, a forgiveness that could be granted only by God.
However unsure I was about the existence of God, I also knew that
I could not lie to God.

In retrospect, I find it extremely difficult to describe the pain
of discovering that gap between the two worlds and to explain that
this was something that really preoccupied me. I could not talk to
my parents, because they constituted the other side. All the growing
pains, the feelings of power and joy, of humiliation and vindication
in early youth took part in this double play of the worlds pitted
against each other.

I knew that these two elements had to get on speaking terms within
me. I thought that one day I would have to choose between them.
And then I probably would choose the world of my peers, because
that seemed to me the obvious, straightforward way to live and
argue. But that would be to deny the crucial part of my parents'
world which I knew also to be true, though it was somehow
secret, storylike, difficult, complex. I had no words with which to
communicate it.

Still, in 1975, I did not know how much I feared the past until
my mother told me on my birthday that my father had called up
some of my old classmates and that they were coming over for tea.
I became stiff with fear to have to face the past. As in a time-
machine the scene quickly comes into view: classroom, stomachache,
"hope I don't get questioned, since I don't know where we are,"
sitting at the last desk at the row next to the window, thinking:
"If God exists, shouldn't it make a difference? If I break a rule,
what will he do?"

But to explain all this, I had better begin with Monika: I fell
in love with her when I was ten years old. She came into the
classroom wearing a light beige dress with a full skirt and a tight

bodice. Her slim legs and arms were deeply tanned, and her hair was bleached from the sun. Her nose was Roman, and her eyebrows met right in the middle of a wonderful, round face with a small strawberry mouth. Her hands and feet were tiny. She looked so outstanding. She was shortwaisted, and she moved in a manner that I instinctively felt was more feminine than the tomboy manners I had unconsciously adopted. When she smiled, her eyes turned very green. I watched her in awe and admiration. I would try anything to catch her attention and to see those eyes turn green.

As a matter of fact, I did not have to work hard to get her attention. But something happened that had never happened to me before. I had lived completely secure within the embrace of my family and, never for a minute, had I doubted its standards. Monika had come from a family with a different set of values, and since these were so much more supported by the general tenor of society, she never had any doubts. It was she who threw me into what became my first crisis which dragged on and developed into a struggle.

At first I did not notice anything at all. I was in a new school and in a new class, and it took time—in fact several years—before a pecking order was established. It never dawned on me that the classroom was a battlefield where all you did and said could be turned against you. I tried to make friends, and I picked the friends from the group that interested me the most. There Monika was the center, and we did make friends.

I tried to be entertaining by telling stories. And when it occurred to me that those stories might be boring, I spiced them with grisly details. Monika stopped me cold by saying, "You are lying." That was the beginning of an awareness but in no way of an understanding. The awareness of shame, of being capable of something unacceptable, of lying.

I began to see the world around me at home and to compare it with the world outside. I was by no means kind to the home world, but my feelings were powerful enough so that I did not accept the outside world wholesale. I began to make distinctions, and I wanted badly to learn and to understand. School did not develop into anything more than just a tolerable drag. To sit with books in front of me in order to learn a few facts by heart made no sense. I turned to fiction and read voraciously. I went through the motions of school, piano lessons, girl scouts. My eyes were not always turned to the windows. I think I observed a great deal in those years, but my consciousness had no proper locker to store things in.

I saw my classmates as through a haze in those days, and I never could see myself objectively. My tendency to both over- and under-estimate myself stems from this period. I loved to be by myself out in the woods. On sunny days I did not want to go to school. I played hooky, cheated, and lied in order to get away, and I was punished for it. I never disputed my punishment. I expected to be punished. I never considered myself as suffering. It was just that I had to make room for myself, and knew no other way than deception. I began to loathe the way I was and wanted to change it.

Those who read Kierkegaard are always astonished by his constant harking back to one incident and the amount of suffering he heaped upon himself from a small event. But I learned from this experience how crazy it is when one is young and sensitive to lose all proportions, to feel all is lost, to struggle between self-assertion and self-condemnation.

❦

I doubt that it would have been such a drawn-out and painful secret affair had I not been subjected to wearing braces on my teeth. Just at the time when teenagers search for themselves and explore with others of their own age group, I was isolating myself more and more because of what I considered an unsightly and hurting face. To have braces in those days was a very painful affair, and I seemed to be the only one who had them. I stopped smiling. The very thing that was devised to make me more beautiful and acceptable in society isolated me the most.

It was my private reading that came to my rescue. Not prose but poetry. One poet in particular, Gunnar Ekelöf, lent "amazing grace," and although I was so young and immature I got great solace from thinking I knew what he meant when he wrote words like these:

> The beauty I've sought was the quiver of the diving-board.
> The wisdom I've believed was the diver's cowardice.
> But he who awaits atonement, he is the unatoned.
> He who wants salvation, he is already damned.

> Denial? No, the deepest faith,
> that shall be attained first when you believe nothing.
> I do not lie, it does not lie in me
> and the truth is far from me (I am far from me).
> I abandon myself
> as the last rat abandons a sinking ship,
> a burning wreck of which the depth gets its part when the
> height has got its share,
> (you're weighed on a scale and found partly light partly heavy),
> shipwrecked, drifting on dark shape-shifting waves,
> attracted and irradiated by the star of the mysterious wrestling,
> she who, though unseen, is mightier than sun and moon,
> she who at the same time is direct and devious, dark and light,
> at the same time! Not one at the time.
> Life is a meeting of contrasts.
> Life is neither-nor.
> Life is neither day nor night,
> but dawn and dusk.
> Life is neither an evil nor a good;
> it is the grist between stones.

I took that message to heart. I embraced it. I did not have to pretend or defend. I could be just myself. I could start just where I was, from zero, from scratch. I could go slow. That became an enormous relief. A new beginning.

Presently I came up with a brilliant idea which would please my family as well as give me a breather and prolong the resumption of my quest. After school I would go to the university and study theology. That solution made me happy and relieved during my last year in high school. I was naïve enough to think that by studying theology I would get to know God.

Twenty-five years later the news reached me that Monika had died. I was shocked. I had nourished the hope that one day we would meet as adults. Why was *I* plodding along? The school years returned for a while to my memory, and when I was home on a short visit, I met with a few of the old classmates. But it was not fun. The old pecking order re-established itself at once. I was particularly badly off, since I now had to defend United States policy and explain what seemed to them indefensible. In the course of the evening I even got the feeling that they thought I had become a Fascist, an anti-Semite, an imperialist of culture and business. Driving home that night without having dared to talk to them about Monika, I vowed to myself never to look them up again. It was no use. At such reunions the past was spread too thick to let the present get a chance. And the past was heavy for me.

So on my fiftieth birthday—on the very day that I had happily dreamt would be a lovely reunion of my family from America with my family in Sweden—an amazing surprise was arranged for me. The period of my life that I would be most happy to forget and had relegated to the bottom of a bottomless sea was now to be walking in through the door in just a few hours. All my capacity for feeling was drained away; I was numb.

When I first saw some of my classmates, I was, after all, delighted. How nice of them to come! But I was also terrified: school had been endlessly boring yet full of pressure, as I had experienced it. Making conversation over tea and cake did in no way dispel my terror; I felt like a cowardly Christian before the lions. Here sat the inquisition before a tiny heretic. Of course, I was at fault and had the wrong attitude. I had conjured up a horrible memory of school and of merciless schoolmates whose measuring sticks constantly wanted to eliminate something which was in me. Nothing during the whole sabbatical year was for me so privately painful as this unexpected confrontation with a past that I had shoved into a closet.

I believe that our children have this advantage over us: the split between the two worlds, that of the "believers" and that of the "unbelievers," is no longer so gaping. Today nobody is sure. We are all aware that we are believers—whether we believe in wisdom and rationality by holding the door closed against irrationality and chaos, or whether we peek through the cracks. We know much more about our biases, and our children are not starting out so high on the ladder bias built.

ꑭ

Power and lack of power. When we have reached an understanding of the importance of these two concepts by observing their workings in ourselves and in institutions, then we have the key to much strange behavior that we might not have been able to explain before.

All literature is about power: who has it, who is out to get it, who is in charge, who wishes to distribute wealth and wisdom, and who wants to redress grievances and reach a new balance? In a power struggle, bearing witness to our neighbor is the challenge. True or false. In order to reinforce our own power we often unwittingly bear false witness. In order to look a little better myself, I talk down my neighbor. In order to make my own country seem the stronger and more justified, as well as my own people, my own race, my own religion—even my own sex—I simplify and distort the record of "my neighbor."

We grow up and live with ideas which we never challenge but cherish. And in order to make them even more attractive and shine the more, we downgrade others. This happened in the course of the history of Christianity. We downgraded other religions, calling them polytheistic, animistic, crude bargaining, etc., in order to have our own brand seem superior. During the eighteenth and nineteenth centuries, people became quite good at naming religions, ordering them on a value scale with Christianity at the very top. These were also the centuries of rampant nationalism. Textbooks were written and distributed for the first time not only to the few within the university community but to the many all over the land. Each country developed a ferocious feeling of its own worth, and even of the worth of each region within the country. I remember when I once asked a student if he knew any European history, he answered that he was from Texas. When I looked a bit surprised, he said that in Texas they had given him a choice of either world history or Texas history. "And," he said, "since Texas history seemed shorter, I chose that."

In Sweden we read Swedish history and world history; the time allotted was the same for each. A one-to-one relationship. Thus I grew up with a strong sense of how superior Sweden was to other countries. To this day I may gloat over the fact that Sweden has the highest living standard in the world and quite an equitable distribution of the national income, while in the United States only a lucky 10 per cent receives more than one quarter of the national income and a mere 20 per cent owns 80 per cent of all private wealth. I refute the argument often heard in the United States that with all the equality in Sweden there cannot be much incentive to produce. That is not true. The Swedes produce eleven times more in growth rate than do the Americans. Although Sweden has the most comprehensive social welfare system in the world, the Swedish industrial system outperforms the United States competitive system. There is no contradiction between government intervention and growth. Lack of planning and social spending causes waste in the United States. But why do I say this when I know that it will make people so angry, and that they will finally tell me that Sweden does not count. A small country cannot teach a big one.

Power is most interesting. What it does to peoples' eyes and perceptions of their concepts of right and wrong, true and false. When Henry Kissinger was at Harvard I sat in on one of his courses. Later I met him at a dinner. I remember him as a short, chubby man who bit his fingernails and whose slow, porridgy manner of speech, with its heavy German accent, made one quite drowsy. He spoke of such gruesome subjects as "war by proxy" and "the delicate balance of power." He was not in power then—this being in 1968 when Robert Kennedy was calling on the Harvard liberals. Kissinger, a Rockefeller man, was not visited. From the dinner I remember him as a witty man with a humorous glint in his eye that seemed to hint at an underlying compassion. After dinner he sat on a sofabed that did not allow his short legs to reach the floor. So he curled up and seemed quite cozy.

When President-Elect Nixon called Kissinger to Washington, I wondered how the press would let him fare. But power intervened. It threw an instant mandorla around his person. His accent was thrilling. His charm unequaled. The playboy of the Western world. His style of secrecy mixed in with intimate revelations, leaks from a senior official, was hailed as diplomacy. His obvious lies were excused, since he was a Harvard professor who must have his delicate ulterior motives. Kissinger served Nixon's bluff faithfully. Yet he always managed to keep himself apart: a lovable teddybear, the most brilliant Secretary of State. Now he is writing his memoirs. Of course we will read them. The play is fascinating.

Power turns our values askew. What family, for instance, would or should be allowed to perpetuate its fortune and fame by being able to dictate its own policies the way the royal families of Europe once did? To inherit power is very dangerous. Once upon a time the eldest boy interited the family name and the family estate. We have now come to the conclusion that this was to wrong the other children. When will we realize that to inherit the family firm and fortune is to wrong the people who have invested their life in that work? They too are partners. They have the right to a fair share of the yield. Feudalism is gone. The upstairs-downstairs world was what the immigrants thought they had left behind; and yet here in the United States we have more inequality than in most Western societies. The power of money has turned people's eyes. They see only the glory and revel vicariously in it. They nourish the hope of reaching the top, and therefore they refuse to acknowledge the inequality inherent in the system.

Kissinger made it. Rockefeller used him and gave him to Nixon. But in the end he made it for himself. We forget at what price to the country. In particular those who call themselves "most patriotic" forget that price.

✿

The other day I pulled the history book from the bookshelf—the one we used in Sweden when I went to school. I was fascinated by the way it interpreted history. We learned history in chronological layers: the Egyptians, Babylonians, Greeks, Romans. And that is the end of Antiquity. Then follow the dark Middle Ages with their emperors East and West and a smattering of the Arabs and Islam. The rise of the pope and the fall of pope and emperor with the emergence of the national states, England and France. Already on page 135 we are dealing with the ambitious couple, Ferdinand and Isabella, who, among many other things, also kicked the Arabs out of Europe in 1492.

In the light of present developments in Africa, South America, and Spain, it is precious to read these sparse sentences: "The only important part of the peninsula not belonging to Spain was Portugal, one of the Christian minikingdoms created during the fight against the Arabs. Furthermore, up in the Pyrenees a tiny independent kingdom, Navarra, was proclaimed."

Then follow Italy and the Renaissance, the Reformation and counter-Reformation, the fall of Spain and the rise of Holland, and then the religious wars.

The sun rises with Louis XIV who presently will meet resistance from the British. Enlightenment arrived; Prussia wants to become

Germany, while France and England get busy colonizing. Russia is opening windows, and Poland is divided. Time for revolution. The nineteenth century, "l'ancien regime," falls apart in different ways all over Europe, and a military dictator crowns himself emperor. When Napoleon fell, that empire fell with him. People now taste freedom, and it tasted better than expected. After the collapse there was a meeting in Vienna to rearrange and stabilize Europe. According to my book, written by Grimberg-Jacobson–Tunberg, the Alliance worked according to three principles: (1) legitimacy, (2) the creation of buffer states in order to guard against renewed French expansion, (3) the balance of power.

If this sounds somewhat familiar, maybe you would be interested in what we learned about Metternich: "Metternich was an unblinking enemy to all movements of liberation and his views for a while determined the policy of the great powers. Now and then representatives of these (countries) met at congresses where they discussed the affairs of Europe and decided on intervention as soon as any revolutionary movement showed up. The great powers wielded a ruthless guardianship over the small nations."

Domestically a growing animosity began to spurn all reforms and spread a distrust of the will of the people. There were persecutions against spiritual and political liberation movements and censorship against publishing. This happened particularly in Austria and the German states. People were even thrown into jail. But the liberation movements were not to be hindered, and thus we get the messy end of the nineteenth century and the bloody beginning of the twentieth.

My book speaks proudly and unblushingly of the colonial time and of the beginning of the imperial U.S.A. From Spain, the United States got Cuba, Puerto Rico, Hawaii, the Philippines, and Haiti, and put a lot of pressure on Brazil, Argentina, and Chile, which, however, kept their independence. In order to get quickly from one ocean to the next, the Americans conquered and built in Panama the famous canal. Why not? The British had conquered and built the Suez. This is the one paragraph devoted to the U.S.A. in the era after World War I:

The United States. The policy of the United States has been markedly non-interventionistic ever since the war. After Wilson there were a couple of presidents from the Republican party, but the new president, elected in 1932, F.D. Roosevelt, is a Democrat.

Thus endeth my history book from high-school days. That summary treatment of the United States was typical of our education which emphasized SWEDEN and her allies. Where the American Revolution and George Washington were dealt with in 3½ pages, the French Revolution and Napoleon had 30 pages. There is some consolation in the fact that the Russian Revolution, with Lenin and Stalin, were allotted a single page. It is all very relative, and when Nixon speaks of getting into the history books, we presume he means a favorable mention in the American ones. That the Vietnamese, Cambodian, or Indian ones will also mention him is certain.

Not to distort the records of our own personal life, not to distort our own national history, not to distort the possibilities of the future—that is what is asked of us. And that is a near impossible task. But we can strive for it by considering our neighbors, and by being as true to them as we want to be to ourselves. To put ourselves in their shoes and feel them pinch.

CHAPTER 9

Love Your Neighbor as Yourself

1954. After a summer made mellow and poignant by the impending separation, Krister flew ahead of the rest of the family, while I packed our meager belongings and put them into storage. I left the children with my parents in Stockholm and returned once more to Uppsala for my last exam in one hectic, impossible week, when every old friend had to be seen and conversations were made incoherent because the future was a huge cloud without shape. I knew that the following week I would have to face that future. The world of the known and well-worn would disappear.

Very early two weeks later, I stood on the deck of the Swedish oceanliner, trying to discern the Statue of Liberty with my children holding onto me. It had been a rough crossing and we had been forced to stay inside the whole time. Because of the children I had little chance to make contact with other passengers. In any case they all seemed older and hard of hearing—to judge from the many hearing aids I saw peeking out from under white frizzy hair or below grey-speckled crewcuts. The overwhelming majority of these people were Swedish-Americans, and they loved to try their Swedish on me. So we talked about trivia: *Stockholm, vackra stad; Småland, många vackra flicka; Mamma from Norrland; Pappa Värmland;* moster has a good life; faster has a good family. While we talked, I observed their hands and legs. In most cases it was obvious that these people had worked hard in their lives; since this effort had to be justified, I was not surprised when they began clanking on Sweden's socialist government ard its bureaucracy and continued by saying that Sweden was a godless country. America was the land of the free. The land of opportunity. God's country. When I lamely tried to contradict them, they smiled and said, "You'll see!"

When they learned that we were going to Harvard, they became apprehensive. "Harvard is Communist," said more than one. Senator McCarthy had just been censured but the majority of the passengers were from the Middle West and what they remembered was that Harvard had spoken out against their senator *and* patriotism.

In a few hours we would be in New York. Krister would meet us and we would go straight to Cambridge to settle into our new house, the second and third floor of a Cambridge "villa." Out of the mist rose the skyline, and when finally, at considerable distance, we passed the Statue of Liberty, I knew that in more than a trivial manner we had made an important crossing. And it was also hot, terribly hot with no possibility of changing, since everything was packed and had to be checked out. My ankles swelled. My face became beet red from heat and nervousness. The children were angels, but they too were overwhelmed and took off their coats innumerable times while we passed from one checkpoint to the next. Finally, after hours in line, we were on land. And there came Krister. We fell all over him. In the big, bustling, dirty, scary world of New York, we had found each other. I held onto him as the children had to my skirt.

During those hours of immigration, I don't recall that I was able to muster a thought. It was all checking, counting, lifting, moving, and looking out for the children. Their strongest impression was that America had Black people such as they had never seen before.

☙

That was the beginning. It took us twelve years before we applied for United States citizenship. It is hard to leave a small country for a big one. The main reason for our final decision was the children. They had grown up here. We had formed a family here which was more familiar to them than the kind of dreamlike family they had in Sweden, represented by letters in the mailbox, photos on the wall, and packages for Christmas and birthdays. The Swedish family had become a mental picture whereas the American family was a daily reality. A family is usually not a conscious thing but something that just is. It works when there is a crisis. America gave us friends who functioned as if they were relatives.

Then there was also the very practical question of where you pay taxes. If your money is constantly working in one kind of society, should you not identify with it? And vote?

But nothing pushed us for making up our minds about citizenship so much as the Vietnam War issue. For me at home, alone, the war was on my mind at all hours of the day. The first thing in the morning when the Today Show woke me up and one senator or another commented on the latest development, I began to speak back, reminding them of the origin of the war and of this country's traditions. Thus I came down to breakfast all wound-up. Driving the children to school with the blare of awful music on the radio, now and then interrupted with the news of the body count, and coming home to a cup of coffee and the paper in solitude and quiet, the long dialogue with the unresponsive partner continued.

We lived here, we liked it here, we worked here, and brought up our children like other American children. Our boys were approaching draft age. "On this the happiest day of your life," said the material which was given to us when we received United States citizenship. I thought, "How antiquated, certainly this was not going to be the happiest day of our lives!" We had struggled with the decision for years. Should we or should we not become Americans? We lived here, earned our living here, our children were growing up here. Yet our roots and our memories and education and values were Swedish. The decision was grueling. To be swallowed up in this huge country. To have sons of draft age.

❦

Here we were. It was January, 1967. The courtroom was crowded with people and an anxious atmosphere. The paneled walls, the high ceiling, and tall windows seemed indifferent to all the little people moving about on the floor, trying to find the right place to sit and never really settling down. They seemed to ask themselves if all the requirements had been filled, if all the permits and recommendations were properly filed, and if their names were on the list of those who today were going to be sworn in as United States' citizens. There still seemed to be some last-minute business. The resident alien cards were to be turned in. When we entered, we were whisked away to specially designated chairs because our son had refused to swear that he would "bear arms." He was now to be asked to swear this special oath of loyalty. Right away I was gripped by the tension in the room, and it did not abate when an official approached us and asked if we were Lutherans. When we confirmed that that was the case, he shook his head, muttering, "I know that Jehovah's Witnesses do these things, but Lutherans—never." Looking around, I saw several young men in uniform; the knowledge that their processing for citizenship had been eased by their willingness to go into military service did not diminish my tension. The country was at war, an undeclared war in Vietnam. At any time now our son could be called. Citizen or non-citizen. He was willing to serve in the military but not to bear arms, and soon now he would have to stand up and bear witness to his conviction.

The judge had not yet entered, and I had time to observe the other citizens-to-be. The majority—though neatly dressed for the occasion—were wearing inexpensive clothes. Their shoes especially gave away their status as immigrants who had started on the low rung. They were "working people" who had found jobs, friends, and a way of life, and they were anxious to stabilize, improve, and settle in this country. The overwhelming majority that day were white, but by no means Anglo-Saxon or Protestant-Puritan. I heard sounds of unrecognizable languages, and it must have been the same for the others who heard us whisper to each other in Swedish. We had no idea of what actually was going to take place, except that, at some point, we would have to swear an oath of loyalty to the United States in which we promised to forswear any other power, prince, or potentate.

The judge entered and a hush went through the assembly. Soon enough we were at the loyalty oath, and our son was called to stand up in front of all the people. He was the one and only who had reneged on the "bearing of arms" clause. Despite his steady, clear voice, and good Scandinavian frame, he looked frail and vulnerable. After him came our turn, the masses, to "repeat after me." Thus, citizenship was bestowed upon us. But before we could pick up our papers, the judge gave a speech. He began by referring to our son's oath and said that here in this courtroom we had seen and heard what it means to be an American. It means to stand up for one's own conviction, to speak one's mind in freedom without fear. Furthermore, he wanted to impress on us that from that moment on we were full-fledged citizens of the United States. No longer were we apprentice-citizens but first-rate citizens with a very special task. Since the United States in recent decades had become involved in foreign affairs all over the world—a novel situation for this country, heretofore so self-contained and protected by oceans—what this country now needed was people who did know other countries firsthand and who could help to further the understanding of foreign countries. "You have a knowledge that we sorely lack and it is your duty to speak up," said he, "and tell us how other people live, think, and feel."

Finally he reminded us that this country was the amalgamation of many races, traditions, creeds, and beliefs. All sorts of people had been welcomed. Only the Blacks had been brought here by force to do the lowliest work. And only recently had the Blacks been permitted to enter the competitive labor market and to fend for themselves. But society had by no means given them an equal chance. In order to make America what she wanted to become, we should be aware of this bias and discrimination and help to overcome the curse.

I listened to the speech; and with every breath and sentence I grew happier and prouder of having finally taken the step to join the community where we live. America is a faith in the human possibility to overcome. The Bill of Rights is a ticket to a better world. When we finally received our papers and were about to leave the courtroom, I was in such a euphoric state that I could have embraced the nice little lady in her American Legion hat, with hand outstretched to be the first to congratulate us on this "the happiest day of our lives." At that moment the presence of the Legion did not strike me as odd.

That night our friends and neighbors and sponsors threw a party for us and we spoke of all the details and we laughed and we hugged. We ate and drank and talked seriously. And when we finally walked home, we felt that indeed it had been "the happiest day."

The judge's name was Arthur Garrity.

During the dark winter months it happens, when something is difficult and the world seems to turn against me, that I stop wherever I am or whatever I am doing and I think, "How long is it now before I can get to Nantucket?" And I get comfort because it can never be more than seven months at the most. For a person like myself, who has waited years to see her homeland, that is not a very long time.

Nantucket is where we go in the summer. It is a tiny island, a heaving breath from the bottom of the ocean, a sand castle of exquisite though modest beauty, a gem with precarious ecological balance that has become a toy of the twentieth-century affluent. One day it will be washed away—lost to the sea.

We came to Nantucket in the beginning of the sixties. And, like almost all others, we fell in love with the endless beaches, the dunes, the moors, the clear blue sky, the friendly fog, the quaint houses, and the cobblestone streets—all, in short, that you now read about in the tourist pamphlets and hear advertised over radio and TV. But to us Nantucket became much more. When Krister became Dean and we began to live in the deanery across the street from the school where students, faculty, and staff—if they were not in the house—were just outside the window, I then said to Krister, "Let's get a place where we can get away, where we can be alone, where we are free to make fools of ourselves." And we both knew in that instant that it meant Nantucket. We were lucky, because wonderful friends sold us, practically gave us, a corner piece of their property, and on that land we raised a prefab house that fit us like a glove. The house and the land came as close to being an idol as anything in our life. It was on Nantucket that we could breathe and rest with each other. There was time without demands. As soon as we sat down on the ferry, we could see it beginning to happen. We had grabbed chairs without even looking to see who else was on board. We smiled faintly at those who fed the sea gulls, while we wiped the crumbs from our hands after having consumed our sandwiches and swallowed the last sip of beer before settling down to sleep. When we arrived in Nantucket harbor, we were already groggy from our first two hours of sleep. When we then entered the house, it did not take long before the first jubilant inspection trip ended in the bedroom—and more sleep. Days began early out of habit, but after grass or hedge clipping, wood sawing, lunch, and swimming, we were back in bed again—only to wake up for dinner, enjoy it, and fall back into bed again. Krister needed a few days of this before he regained human proportions. These were days when we saw no one but each other, hardly talked save for mutterings or happy exclamations. Days when we cleaned the house, spruced up the yard, and tended to each other and slept—and slept. After a few days we perked up. Our color changed to bronze, and our wrinkles looked like happy white quick worms.

The food we ate was raised, picked, caught, and made right there: bluefish, swordfish, clams and plaice; fresh Portuguese bread fetched by Krister from the bakery at 7:30 each morning; unsalted butter, carrots, peas, cauliflower, broccoli, lettuce, basil, mint, and new, new potatoes; blueberries, blackberries, and homemade ice cream.

Of course this table of abundance had to be shared. Our children, grandchildren, and friends able to appreciate the luxury of simple things were invited. With them we have had the loveliest picnics on shores and moors, the greatest discussions, in the mornings combined with Scripture reading, the most open-ended after-dinner gab. With these friends we have seen the worst as well as the greatest movies. As a rule none of us knew anything about movies; so to roll the dice and go was a favorite pastime.

Together we took up projects like building a shed, fixing a door, embroidering a pillow, knitting a sweater. And together we rejoiced in the finished product. Amazing how much praise one can spill on a shed built by a professor. A shed perhaps more useful than many a *Festschrift!*

We knew practically nobody on Nantucket, and that has its advantages: no cocktail parties, no chitchat, no obligations, no students asking questions or wanting to prove something, no papers to read, no noise. Alone or together with our friends we lived our quiet, undisturbed life.

We were in sovereign command over our little piece of paradise. Of course we heard and saw Nantucket on its way to being wrecked and polluted. This we mourned and sighed about, but our private little spot still stood intact. Walk out of our back door and there was not a house in sight—only marvelous greenery; a patio where we didn't need a stitch of clothing; a hedge where a pheasant couple lived; a thicket out of which a rabbit jumped now and then; birdsong—almost too loud in early morning; hydrangeas and marigolds providing the Swedish colors during August. The Big Dipper stood right above our "pond" at night, so that when we returned from night swims in the phosphorescent waters, we could shower, gazing at the familiar constellation. We were absolutely alone. We, the stars, and all nature. Did we love all and everything in those moments!

On our return from the sabbatical we learned that our private hideaway, "our" Nantucket, was no longer going to be the same. We were going to acquire a neighbor: a house would be built right next to our patio—no more than fifteen yards away. Our world would fall apart. We were losing something enormously dear and important. I grieved, and at the same time I was angry at myself for my selfishness. Across the street we had had neighbors from the beginning. I could hear them at night and I could see them come and go. We said "hello." But "our" side had been quiet. The moors had a small extension right behind us, right in that corner where the sun set above the thicket—right where the new house was now to be built. What seemed ironic was that it was *I* who had introduced our prospective neighbors to Nantucket. They had come as our guests and we rejoiced that they seemed to appreciate this place to the full.

But now they were to be here for good. We would be stuck with each other—which meant we would really have to learn to love one another. Love your neighbor as yourself.

And it worked. Not because of me—as can be clearly seen from what I have just written—but because of Ole. He enthusiastically built his own house with his own hands. But he did much more: he created a neighborhood, a community. He explored the island and let all of us rediscover it with him. His nature and personality were such that nobody dreaded his intrusion; soon we all trusted him and came to be prepared for him to appear when we least expected. Suddenly he would be at the door with crabs he had caught—wanting us to share; or he would sneak into the pew next to us in church; or climb the roof to take a picture; or fix the gutter; or take us swimming and berrypicking when we were tired; or encourage me to write when I felt it was useless; or tell a story that would make us chuckle. And we all marveled at what he accomplished and what we accomplished with his help. It is not true that one human being is another one's wolf. Ole proved to me that a human being can be another one's angel. With his coming, Nantucket changed from past to present tense. What we had built selfishly Ole built unselfishly. And therefore Nantucket is so much more valuable for us now than it once had been. It is not a quaint getaway, it is a way of life.

The first time I met Ole was when he was a student in 1969— just at the time when University administrators had developed a mistrust of students. Ole had come to the door which I opened somewhat reluctantly and he asked if I would keep some of his paintings while he was away in Europe for a year. All during that period his paintings cheered me, and some still do (the ones he gave us). It was a typical Ole-thing to do. In a moment of polarization, he appeared and established trust and cheer.

Thus, I was taught a lesson which has become important for me: it is easy to be generous and to love one's neighbor when one is in command. But when one loses command and is put on an equal footing and even becomes dependent on the other—then comes the test: not to be envious, not to be sulky, not to try to reestablish the hierarchial order. Too often we take what is ours for granted and are taken by surprise when a shrinking world causes intrusions on "our" turf and territory. We want to teach "them" to live their way on their land, and we are disgruntled or dismayed if they live our way on "our" land.

To coexist is not enough of a solution; to interact and to share is the solution. To learn to trust and to love one another. America has been an experiment in the mingling of ethnic groups. Until a decade ago we thought the experiment was working very well: up to that time we still believed in the "land of opportunity." But after that the fact could no longer be denied that opportunity had vanished; sharing had become a necessity. And the wish to share was hard to find, almost absent. The wonderful idea of the melting pot no longer worked its magic, but evaporated. Suddenly we were thrust into warring folds. Many of us were caught in the crossfire.

We saw fear and we listened to how people were groping for models, "This is like the thirties in Germany or like the early fifties during the McCarthy era." But it was neither. When a new situation occurs, people become frightened and they instinctively call for law and order. Fathers become afraid of their sons and sons of their fathers. Ole taught us that the stranger who comes to the door may be our saving angel.

CHAPTER 10

What Became of Our Sabbatical?

What became of our sabbatical? Was it just another year during which we traveled and rested, ate and drank, read and wrote and filled the wastebasket? Was it a success or a failure?

The first of May we were back in Uppsala. Krister had been eager to get back and work on his commentary. We had rented two student rooms in order to make the last finishing stretch so that he could return with a manuscript, a visual piece of evidence that the sabbatical had paid off. The weighty item in our return luggage. On the 15th of May Krister called me in to his study and I knew right away from the manner in which he asked me to be there that he had something significant to say. When I sat down I anticipated the seriousness in his voice. Then he told me that he had come to the conclusion that he should scrap his work on his commentary on Romans. I felt terrible, drained, and didn't know what to say. He had worked for many years on this project for which he once had received an advance from the publisher. The sabbatical had begun in hope of fulfilling that obligation. Much time was spent in libraries and at the desk in order to meet all the scholarly expectations in producing a comprehensive, yet sharply focused survey of the significance of that epistle. The lectures he had given on the continent had conveyed the mastery he had reached over the material. And now—the more he had sorted his notecards and the more he wrote—the more he felt uncertain, impatient, and frustrated. The subject was already saturated. Every verse, word, and comma were commented on and theorized over. There was too much for any commentator to absorb. The material had accumulated from commentary to commentary. A German commentary had just been published which was inclusive in a judicious way. The question was, "Should he spend his time ahead scrutinizing this one, trying to come up with variations or should he act on his notion that this kind of scholarship had reached a point of diminishing return and scrap his own effort?" Scholarship is not just for the club. Influx from and outflow to the contemporary world warrants its renewal. Krister

119

had always argued that in biblical criticism the time has come to return to the texts themselves, finding their original message, understanding how they were meant and how they were heard in their entirety, drawing upon the wealth of philosophical, historical, and archeological knowledge we have gained in re-creating their original poignancy. This was what he had done in his lectures.

At first I felt thunderstruck. Was not this an acknowledgement of defeat and the aim for the year forfeited? All that labor in vain! I wondered how I could comfort him.

But he was no longer sorry. Rather the decision to scrap the project relieved him. After he had written to the publisher and returned the advance money his only regret was that it had taken so long to make the decision. (Two years later a totally different book built on his lectures appeared.)

We began to pack up. I spent some time with my parents and I tried to go very slowly although I was living more in anticipation of the return than in the moment of farewell. One of the very last things I did before leaving Sweden was to go to Sigtuna where Gunnar Ekelöf, the poet who has increasingly meant more and more to me, had lived during the last years of his life. I went to visit his widow. Together we looked at his books and listened to his voice on tape. To sit in the same room where he had worked was for me an unforgettable and almost incredible event. I have earlier witnessed to his influence on me at an early age. During my years of teaching I had often used his poems and marveled at their impact on students, even in translation. Over the years I had translated quite a few of his poems. Those poems had been created right in this room.

In the Fall, after our return, it occurred to me that I could hand-set and print myself a selection from these translations, beginning with the earliest poems and moving rapidly forward to those written shortly before his death in 1968. It took me almost a year to execute this project but I have seldom enjoyed my work more.

Scholarship is a curious thing. It is part hard work with facts and part imagination. People quibble about the percentages, but not about the mix. To me it is fascinating to see where it takes us and how it moves us about. The sabbatical with lazy time makes the imagination fertile to produce its magic trick.

Virginia Woolf names it "no-time" and Fredrika Bremer calls the same thing "not-life": the hours, days, weeks, and years we spend feeling unfulfilled, anxious, not doing what we are supposed to do, not living up to our potential. The time when envy is sneaking in and clouding our thoughts and feelings, paralyzing our ability to enjoy what we are doing and leaving us to ruminate over lost opportunities. Loose time when memories haunt us because we let them grow to giant proportions and gain crushing weight. Humor which we so value in others is not allowed to bring its divine healing to our frightened selves. Envy and guilt push us to the brink. Such useless days, weeks, and years. Many of us recognize the paralysis and would do anything to dispel the distress if only we knew how.

There is in fact an opposite to "no-time," and that can be called "eternity." While "no-time" robs us of life—spreading its gray cloak over past, present, and future, "eternity" engages us in life. Both the sabbatical year and Nantucket are experiences that help me understand this. They take us out of circulation to feel the impact of life—not abstractly, but in actual encounters with one another, with others, and with past and future mingled into an active *now time.*

When I get pangs of nostalgia for Sweden I never transport myself to the city and very rarely inside a house. No, it is always walking down a dirt road in hot summer, with ditches on both sides and flowers to pick. Wild strawberries on a thread of grass presented to mother as she sits in the lilac arbor having coffee and freshly baked buns. Or skiing downhill at dusk after school in new snow that lights the dark, wets the woolen mittens, and tastes like dessert. Or picking cherries with my cousins climbing up high, so high that I am afraid to look down. Or—I could go on forever without even beginning to mention the meadows and the birches and the *linnea borealis.* My homesickness is strong, but I know that what I miss is not Sweden, my homeland, but the Sweden where I grew up. It is childhood and youth I long for and that nostalgia is present as well in others who never left to go anywhere. It is not so that I have been bereft of my country. It is only that I have left childhood and youth behind, and these things will never return except in memory. I will never feel for Nantucket's blackberries what I felt for the raspberries of Sörmland.

But there is a Sweden that I miss and which, in my mind, has become a utopia. The small country that had a friendly revolution. A country where people decided that they wanted to share and share alike. Nobody should have to be disadvantaged because he or she was poor. Everybody should have the right to be fed and clothed. Nobody should fear to be sick. Everybody should have free access to hospitals and nursing care. Everybody should have the opportunity to higher learning. The old and crippled should have special privileges since they had to suffer special drawbacks. Equality was a goal that took a heavy toll in terms of taxes, but the majority of the people felt that this was right, and paid.

During the sabbatical we slowly began to discover that this Sweden was no longer. Like a sunken Atlantis that magnificent experiment, unique in history and forty years of age, was billowed over by the waves of world development and the quirks of economics. From the many discussions with friends we understood that the Sweden we loved was now memory and no more vision. So we can never go back.

☙

Every time I visit home Mother at one point says, "Come here, girl." She runs her fingers over my face lightly and then she says, "You have aged." I used to be embarrassed by this ceremony and jokingly shrug it off until I understood what was going on.

Mother had accompanied us that first time we went down to Gothenburg to board the oceanliner for America. Over and over she has told me how well she remembers the three blue figures standing on deck waving to her until they were merely little dots that melted into the horizon. I think that this must be how she still feels today. We have gone away from her. So strong was the emigrant phenomenon in her generation that this was like death itself. For her we will always stand there waving while the ship pulls out and the distance between us rapidly grows until we are gone. In her memory I am always the young mother and the children always small.

I think of the magnificent emigrant epic written by the Swedish author Vilhelm Moberg. There this image is pictured in the reverse. The emigrating couple, Karl-Oskar and Kristina, will always see before their inner eyes the sight of his parents standing at the gate to the old homestead as the horse pulled the carriage loaded with the emigrants and their America chest. There they stood immobile, unsmiling, and staring. The carriage turns a curve and for eternity the parents remain at that same spot never to be seen again but always to be remembered just as in that moment of parting.

When Moberg was interviewed about his work on the Swedish emigrants he said that he had undertaken it because it had played such a role in his own family and in the community where he grew up. Then he added that the vast material had been untouched by the first generation of those who remained because, he thought, for them the subject was simply too close, too touchy, too painful.

Few books that I have read have been so helpful to me as those by Moberg in understanding the America to which we arrived. Through him I understood why America *must* be the best and Americans constantly seek reassurance that it is so. Too much has been at stake, too much has been suffered and sacrificed. It cannot be allowed to fail. Little things, too, that seemed crazy got their explanation. Why, for instance, the Swedish-Americans drink so much coffee, why they mix Danish and sausages for breakfast, why they are fiercely church-affiliated, why they dress in pink, etc., etc. All those things that struck us in the fifties got their historical and sociological explanation in the most human and humorous manner. Had I not read Moberg I would have said Ugh and Bah and How distasteful, but thanks to him I could smile in recognition and admiration. He writes out of his love for America and the Americans and the glorious history that forged the people of immigrants together. The fight for survival and the yield from both land and people.

But that America, too, is a sunken Atlantis. This was plainly and painfully visible when Moberg's work came as a film in the seventies. Beautiful, interminably episodic but without a message, because that message did not fit the time and had therefore been cut by the producers.

Now everything in Sweden, in America, and all over the world is so much more complex. Yet in a way the same. The issue then and now is survival. The investment we had in the near past crumbles and the future is taking shape. In this in-between time we grope for what is basic. Then it is not a bad thing to remember the guideposts we have in the Ten Commandments.

Acknowledgements

Ole Lohensgard read the material in its confusion, advised, and helped me to put it into shape. Louise A. Pfeiffer typed the manuscript with attention and made numerous felicitous improvements. Ingalill Hjelm edited the book with wonderful care and professional skill. With the support of these three friends, I got through to the final product.

Cambridge, Massachusetts   Brita Stendahl
January, 1980